ICE & MIXED CLIMBING:
Modern Technique

ICE & MIXED CLIMBING:
Modern Technique

Will Gadd

Photography by Roger Chayer

THE MOUNTAINEERS BOOKS

Published by
The Mountaineers Books
1001 SW Klickitat Way, Suite 201
Seattle, WA 98134

The Mountaineers Books is the nonprofit publishing arm of The Mountaineers Club, an organization founded in 1906 and dedicated to the exploration, preservation, and enjoyment of outdoor and wilderness areas.

First edition, 2003

Published simultaneously in Great Britain by Cordee, 3a DeMontfort Street, Leicester, England, LE1 7HD

Manufactured in China

Editor: Paula Thurman
Project Editor: Mary Metz
Cover and Book Design: The Mountaineers Books
Layout: Mayumi Thompson and Peggy Egerdahl
Illustrations: Simon Mentz
Photographer unless otherwise credited: Roger Chayer

Cover photograph: *Will Gadd on Sunday Morning Glumpy, Haffner Creek, Kootenay National Park, Canada*
Frontispiece: *Shawn Huisman on Whimper Wall, Icefields Parkway, Banff National Park, Canada*
Backcover photograph: *Kim Csizmazia on Call of the Curtain, Icefield Parkway, Jasper National Park, Canada*
Illustration on page 100 adapted from "Gripped" Magazine

Library of Congress Cataloging-in-Publication Data

Gadd, Will, 1967-
  Ice & mixed climbing : modern technique / Will Gadd ; photography by
Roger Chayer.— 1st ed.
      p. cm. — (Mountaineers outdoor expert series)
  ISBN 0-89886-769-X (alk. paper)
  1. Snow and ice climbing. I. Title: Ice and mixed climbing. II.
Title. III. Series.
  GV200.3.G33 2003
  796.9—dc22
                          2003014891

Contents

CHAPTER 4
Anchors, Belaying, and Leading

CHAPTER 5
Descending

CHAPTER 6
Advanced Ice Techniques

CHAPTER 7
Leading and Protecting Mixed Routes

CHAPTER 8
Mixed Climbing

CHAPTER 9

Moving in the Mountains in Winter

CHAPTER 10

Systems for Survival

CHAPTER 11

Training for Winter Climbing

Will Gadd on the unformed Fang, Vail, Colorado, USA Photo © David Brooks

Acknowledgments

Thanks to the many earlier ice climbers who developed the techniques, gear, and awareness we all climb with today; all the people who took my clinics (they were really teaching me); Roger Chayer and Mary Metz (without them this book would never have happened); and Ben and Cia Gadd, Kim Csizmazia, Jim Fitzpatrick, Dave Marvin, John Bercaw, Peter Metcalf, Jim Gunning, Dave Bridges, Hayes Wheelless, Jason Macleod, John Winsor, Pete Foster, Mark Twight, Jeff Lowe, Teri Ebel, Scott Semple, Ben Firth, Ueli Steck, Christian Jaeggi, Helgi Christianson, Michael Kennedy and all the other Aspen dogs, and TR Reid.

Special thanks to Nyguen and The Vision climbing gym in Canmore for the gym training photos and a lot of epic training sessions, and to the Bill Warren Training Centre in Canmore for the weight room training photos.

Preface

I started ice climbing over 20 years ago, back in the days when it took a socket wrench or third tool just to place an ice screw. My friends and I often took all day to climb 200 feet of ice, but we laughed often and reveled in the joy of climbing the most unlikely, crazy medium possible: frozen water. Recently I hung upside down in the middle of a 30-foot roof by my heel spurs while my friends and I laughed ourselves silly at the whole situation. Even though the gear and technique have advanced tremendously, the basic joy of winter climbing still fires me up every season like a little kid on Christmas morning. I have won some competitions and put up some hard routes, but grades and achievements are absolutely secondary to good experiences with good people on good climbs.

Over the last five years I've learned a lot about ice and mixed climbing through teaching ice and mixed clinics across North America and in Europe. This book is my attempt to share what I've learned about ice and mixed climbing over the years; I hope these words help you to enjoy winter climbing in your own way as much as I have and for as many years.

NOTE FROM THE PUBLISHER
Safety is an important concern in all outdoor activities. No book can alert you to every hazard or anticipate the limitations of every reader. The descriptions of techniques and procedures in this book are intended to provide general information. This is not a complete text on ice and mixed climbing technique. Nothing substitutes for formal instruction, routine practice, and plenty of experience. When you follow any of the procedures described here, you assume responsibility for your own safety. Use this book as a general guide to further information. Under normal conditions, excursions into the backcountry require attention to traffic, road and trail conditions, weather, terrain, the capabilities of your party, and other factors. Keeping informed on current conditions and exercising common sense are the keys to a safe, enjoyable outing.

—The Mountaineers Books

The Mountaineers Ten Essentials

There are certain items that deserve space in every pack. A climber will not need every one of them on every trip, but they can be lifesavers in an emergency.

1. Navigation (map and compass)
2. Sun protection
3. Insulation (extra clothing)
4. Illumination (headlamp)
5. First-aid supplies
6. Fire (firestarter, matches or lighter)
7. Repair kit and tools
8. Nutrition (extra food)
9. Hydration (extra water)
10. Emergency shelter

CHAPTER 1

Your tools are your life; proper maintenance is critical.

Gear

Modern ice climbing equipment is a beautiful mixture of medieval weaponry and aerospace technology. Hefting a well-balanced ice tool even in the limited confines of a crowded store evokes something primal, perhaps a desire to swing it in the same manner that a long-past ancestor swung a well-balanced branch and thought, "This will do nicely." An employee at Canada's Mountain Equipment Co-op remembers the day a burly member of the Royal Canadian Mounted Police walked into the store and demanded to talk with the "ice-pick" manager. The manager of the ice-tool department appeared, wondering why the RCMP would want to talk with him, and the cop said, "It's about these ice picks you're selling. I can't make them illegal, but I had better never see them in a bar!"

This section outlines the specific functions of ice gear and what to buy to meet those demands. As with all climbing,

the single most important piece of equipment is the gray matter between your ears. Good gear may meet stricter testing standards or perform more reliably, but gear is only as good as the operator.

ICE TOOLS

Ice tools are the single most expensive and critical piece of gear needed for ice climbing other than the climber's judgment (getting good judgment can be very expensive also). A perfect ice tool would swing effortlessly, stick on the first swing every time in any ice, last forever, and feel like an extension of one's nervous system; a good modern tool can come close to these requirements. The first decision a plastic-wielding ice climber on a gear-acquisition bender has to make is what sort of climbing he or she will be doing. This book is primarily about technical

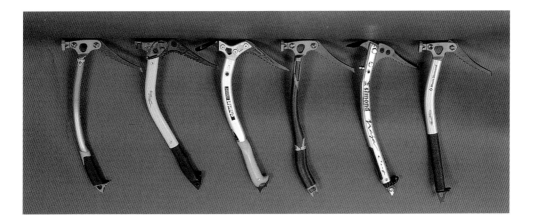

ice and mixed climbing, so I leave out mountaineering ice axes, ski-pole ice axes, and the like. Check out *Mountaineering: The Freedom of the Hills* (The Mountaineers Books, 2003) for that information.

Technical ice tools break down into two varieties: traditional and leashless. Traditional ice tools have a leash system consist-ing of a strap that encircles your wrist, although increasingly they can be modified for leashless use. Climbing leashless is not a new style (Henry Barber and others were playing this game 25 years ago), but only now are manufacturers developing leashless-specific tools. There are already about a half-dozen leashless tools of various stripes on

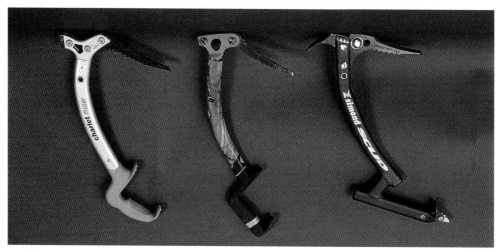

Leashless tools

the market, so understanding the pros and cons of leashless ice climbing is useful for buying decisions.

I climb most multipitch pure ice routes with leashed tools. I've had my feet blow 20 feet above a screw enough times to know the force involved. The impact load on your hands can be quite high without a mechanical assist, and I fear a bad fall may result if I can't hold onto the tool. Add a thick mitt on a cold day or an iced grip and a leash is a prudent bit of safety for leading pure ice climbs, especially if you're a newcomer to the sport. I've seen a few accidents in which climbers fell off and left their well-embedded ice tools in place—with a good leash they would have remained attached to the ice also. Leashless climbing may look cool, but the emergency room isn't.

That said, I do climb ice leashless a fair amount, especially on warmer days with soft ice. I generally prefer a "normal" tool with a leashless adapter for these situations rather than a dual-grip leashless tool. Leashless tools are a tremendous amount of fun and make the same old routes a whole new experience if you've advanced to the point where you need a different challenge.

I prefer to climb hard, mixed routes with leashless tools; the routes are generally steeper and the protection set in such a way that a fall is much safer. Leashless tools are evolving very rapidly, and I may switch to leashless climbing for all climbs in the future, but at this point my leashes still see a lot of use for normal ice climbing.

Some climbers do climb all routes, including alpine routes, leashless; this is a matter of style and personal ethics, both of which are obviously up to the climber and not the author of a book like this. Nothing beats a set of leashless tools and an integrated boot/crampon combination for steep, well-protected mixed routes, and nothing swings like a well-balanced, clip-leash outfitted tool on a multipitch pure ice route. Go leashless if you plan to climb primarily hard mixed routes with good gear; go with a leash-friendly tool that you can attach to a leashless adapter if you plan to climb primarily pure ice. I expect the future of even pure ice climbing will move toward leashless tools and integrated boot/crampon combinations similar to those used for snowboarding, but that day is a way off yet.

TRADITIONAL ICE TOOLS

Any modern tool designed for waterfall ice will get you up any climb out there, but there are major design differences based on what the tool will be used for. Most climbers use two tools of the same design and length from the same manufacturer. Because each design swings and performs differently, it's more efficient to have the same system in each hand. Some climbers carry a third tool in case a pick breaks or if one tool does an impromptu gravity test. This is a good idea, but it adds weight and clutter to your system. Modern picks don't break all that often, and even when they do there's usually enough left to continue climbing at a reduced speed. Prices range from $150 to $300 for a tool with a leash; read magazine reviews and talk to more experienced climbers before investing your money. If possible, attend an ice festival and try out a variety of tools in a variety of conditions. The only way to really determine how well a tool will work is to climb with it in a lot of different conditions.

A very light tool with a lot of clearance will work well when you are climbing ice that has seen a lot of traffic, but it may bounce and not penetrate well on fresh, cold ice. A relatively head-heavy tool with a sharp pick and minimal clearance may work very well on fresh ice, but it might be less effective on a well-climbed route at a popular area with deep holes made by previous climbers. Compromises are in order.

If you plan to climb primarily alpine-style routes, a straighter tool with a steel head (steel heads are better for pounding on while placing the tool into hard snow) is a good bet. If you plan to climb primarily technical ice or mixed routes, then a

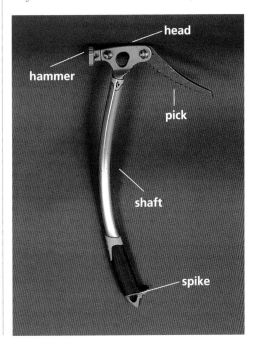

well-designed high-clearance tool is better. If you want to climb everything (and most climbers do), a tool with a steel head and a sufficient but not radical curve is the best bet. Remember that saving a few dollars doesn't amount to much over the three- to five-year life expectancy of a tool. Buy the best and you won't be disappointed.

Traditional ice tools have four main components: the shaft/head, the hammer/adze, the pick, and the leash (unless you're going leashless). All modern tools have a modular design, which means you can combine different picks, hammer/adzes, and leashes with the most expensive part of the tool, the shaft. Any nonmodular tool isn't worth buying for pure ice or mixed climbing; picks wear out relatively quickly.

Shaft/Head. Most climbers prefer a shaft of about 55 centimeters. Small climbers may prefer something a little bit shorter, giants something a bit longer. Shafts come either relatively straight or with some variation of curve. The more well-designed curve a shaft has, the more clearance it will offer for clearing ice mushrooms or other features. However, a large part of an ice tool's accuracy for swinging is determined by how much weight the tool has forward or behind the tool's center of gravity. Tools with radical curves will clear bulges and obstacles with ease but also generally be less balanced and efficient for swinging because so much of the shaft weight is behind the tool's "balance line." A radical curve will also impede the tool's ability to plunge into the snow on ledges or while you are descending from a climb. Many people assume that a moderately curved tool will be useless for plunging into the snow, but it's the radius of the curve that really influences how well the tool will plunge. A tight curve won't plunge at all, but a smooth, large curve will work fine. If you will be climbing only pure ice or mixed routes, plunging ability may be less relevant than the ability to clear ice features.

Most shafts are made from aluminum, most heads from either aluminum or steel. Steel heads are far more durable and generally stronger than aluminum—and also heavier—but this may be a good thing. Total tool weight is easy to measure and a common basis for buying decisions, but pure tool weight is not an indicator of how well a tool will perform in the real world. In fact, the tool's overall balance in combination with the pick design really determines a tool's performance. For a comparison, check out the weight differences among hardware-store hammers: A finishing hammer features a very light, small head while a framing hammer has a relatively massive head. The framing hammer is a more efficient implement for its job despite being heavier. A very light tool with very little weight in the head will often feel great on the shop floor but be nearly useless on a long, steep pitch of cold, hard ice. Testing all the tools on the market is the only way to find out which one works for you.

Pinky rests are a hotly debated topic. I cut them off because they seem to just get in the way, but many climbers find the extra support helpful.

Hammer /Adze. Historically, many climbers preferred to set their tools up with one hammer and one adze. An adze may be useful for chopping steps in hard snow and a few other tricks, but adze-friendly situations are relatively rare on waterfalls or mixed routes. Most modern climbers prefer two hammers; an adze gets in the way far more often than it is useful. However, if you plan to do a lot of alpine climbing, an adze and a hammer will be a good choice. Never climb difficult mixed terrain with an adze on one tool; a number of interesting forehead scars are out there from adzes.

Picks. The shaft/head works in combination with the pick; in fact, the pick angle and shape are as important as the shaft design in determining real-world performance. All manufacturers design their picks to function as a unit with their tools, and picks are not interchangeable among manufacturers for this reason. Most manufacturers make three or four different

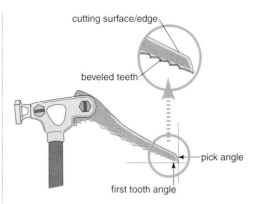

Figure 1. Ice tool with recurved pick

pick designs and leave the final purchase decision up to the consumer. A good shaft with a bad pick can be a liability; a little bit of research on how a company tests its picks, which picks break regularly, and what locals like to run on their tools will really help in choosing a pick/ice tool.

There are three main pick designs: classic, straight, and recurved. I prefer a classic pick for mountaineering and a straight pick for alpine climbing. Recurved picks with larger teeth (see Figure 1) seem to work the best for steep ice and mixed climbing. Thinner picks will generally be easier to place than thicker ones but may not have as good longevity. The steeper the angle of the first tooth, the better the tool will be for hooking in ice or on rock, but too much angle will result in overly sticky picks. See the "Pick Maintenance and Tweaking" later in this chapter for more information on setting your picks up for your style of climbing.

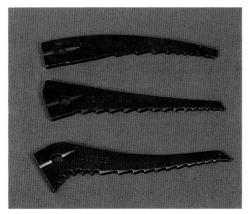

Pick designs: classic, straight, recurved

Tested picks (and tools) are classified as either "B" or "T," and this information is stamped on any pick that has passed one of two tests. T picks have to pass a more stringent test than B picks, but neither test is all that applicable to real-world climbing, in my experience. Still if the pick passes either test, then at least the manufacturer took the time to design its picks reasonably well. Totally uncertified picks from off-brand manufacturers may be great, but quality control and testing are valuable—I'd only buy a tool/pick that passes either of these tests.

Check out how the pick attaches to the tool; some require multiple wrenches, some require only one, and some even allow the climber to use the pick of one tool to remove the pick of the other. No one system is perfect, but I do like simple systems with minimal nuts and bolts to loosen for those times when I have to change a broken pick and I'm a long way from a hardware store. It may be a good idea to buy the same tools as your main partner because that way you don't have to both carry a spare pick and wrench for your individual tool systems.

Leashes. The perfect leash would be completely bombproof when your hand was in it yet would release easily when you wanted it to, never ice up, spread your weight out evenly over your wrist, and weigh nothing. As usual, compromises are in order. How the tool hangs when you let go of it—known as the "hang point"—is determined by the attachment point of the

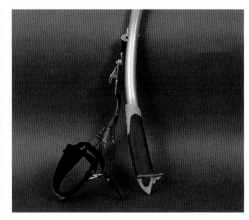

A traditional tool with clipped leash

leash to the tool. A leash threaded through the head of your tool will let the tool hang with the spike straight down at the end of the leash. This hang point will make it difficult to regrab the tool after it hangs and won't help keep your hand close to the tool on steep terrain. It will be great for plunging into the snow though, so most alpine climbers use it. For steep ice it makes more sense to have the hang point closer to the spike on the tool; this helps keep your hand close to the tool when climbing steep terrain, which means you don't have to hang on as hard. Many leashes attach to the head of the tool but allow the climber to adjust the hang point up and down the shaft of the tool. I like this system the best.

No matter what leash you use, be sure that it is set up so that your little finger rests just below the joint between the spike and the shaft when you are hanging from the leash and holding the tool. Most beginning climbers set their leashes up so their little finger is near the bottom of the shaft when they are holding the tool straight on with no glove. When you are hanging from a tool or swinging it, your hand is actually cocked at about a 45-degree angle relative to the shaft; if you set your leashes up for a straight-on grip your little finger will be much too high on the shaft when swinging and hanging, resulting in a seriously impeded swing.

Modern leashes fall into two categories: fixed and clip. Fixed leashes are permanently attached to your tools, while clip leashes, not surprisingly, clip on and off the tool. Fixed leashes are cheaper and lighter and never come unclipped, as clip leashes sometimes can. On the other hand, fixed leashes seldom offer the bomber support and ease of use that clip leashes do. Nothing beats a good clip leash for pure ice climbing, but some people prefer an older-style fixed leash. I like clip leashes that have an adjustable hang point. A fixed stud on the tool limits the climber to only one attachment point, while adjustable clip leashes allow a climber to set the hang point in any position. For steep, pure ice climbing, I like to set the leash so that the tool naturally comes back into my hand when I dangle it. If the route will involve snow traverses or other snow travel, I set the leash so that I can grab the head easily.

Clip leashes allow the climber to easily clip in and out of either tool; this is invaluable when placing a screw. If you start to get pumped on one hand, just clip back in to the other tool and finish the job. Invariably, the sling I want is on the shoulder attached to the tool in the ice, and it's a lot easier to just switch tools and get the sling off than it is to wrestle the tool through the sling or undo a fixed leash, get the sling, and reenter the leash.

Clip leashes take more care and attention than fixed leashes, as the leash may come unclipped from the tool, but most pure ice climbers find the slight risk worth the rewards. Be sure that any clip leash is strong for both a straight-down pull and a more outward pull; some stud-based systems are very weak on the outward pull.

LEASHLESS ICE TOOLS

The current crop of leashless tools developed straight out of the Ice World Cup, where organizers banned leashes to make the routes more difficult. The leashless systems then evolved so quickly that now many people find it easier to climb leashless both on mixed terrain and on more traditional ice. Climbers have now climbed leashless most routes you can think of, from the Rockies classics to long alpine routes around Chamonix. The latest leashless tools are evolving faster than frogs in a radioactive swamp, with comparable mixed results. Be very careful about buying leashless tools; the differences between good and atrocious are much greater than with traditional tools. The only way to really know is to test each brand thoroughly.

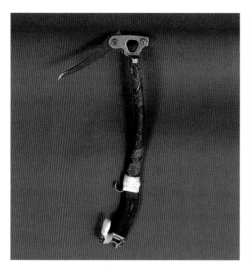

A Cobra™ converted for leashless climbing

Most traditional ice tools can be retrofitted with either clip-on pieces from the manufacturer or with various hardware-store bits and pieces so that they work well for leashless climbing. If you already have a set of ice tools, the simplest solution may be just to copy one of the commercial clip-on designs courtesy of your local hardware store. A traditional tool with a clip-on leashless system often works better for pure ice than a leashless tool; the funky geometry of the new leashed tools often gets in the way for pure ice climbing. However, the leashless-specific commercial tools offer a large improvement for mixed climbing.

The only way to accurately judge the performance of leashless tools is to climb on them in a variety of situations. A good leashless tool should swing reasonably well on pure ice, be comfortable, and offer good support to the hands. Most leashless tools fail one critical test: "grip shift," meaning that the tool radically shifts position when you switch from the lower to the upper grip or back. Grip shift is annoying at best and dangerous at worst; you really need to be able to switch grips safely while climbing mixed terrain ice. You can check for this in the shop: Put the tip of the pick through a sling or on an edge, hang on it, and then switch to the lower grip while still hanging. If the bottom of the handle moves back and forth in an arc of more than about an inch, the tool will not perform well in the real world. Some tools shift up to eight inches and are functionally useless when grabbed on the upper grip. This is a waste of aluminum.

Most climbers will retrofit their tools with sticky tape of some kind to improve grip. Skateboard shops sell the best assortment of grip tape, and hockey tape is also popular. Be sure to use a very tight, thin glove on leashless tools—if your hand can move around inside the glove, then it will when you hang on the tool.

In general, pure leashless tools still lack the precise swing of leashed tools, and most climbers find they work less well for long leads on fresh ice where constant clearing and swinging is required. However, they offer great freedom for placing ice screws and a new world of movement options such as switching hands easily on the tool during traverses and so on. Experiment.

BOOTS

Boots are generally the ice climber's biggest investment after ice tools, so careful thought is in order. Boots are increasingly purpose-built; there is no one boot that will climb well for all uses. Traditionally, plastic double boots were designed to keep your feet warm while climbing acceptably. Leather boots were designed to climb better but with less warmth. Modern ice boots blur these generalizations, but in general plastic boots are warmer and more impervious to water and cold temperatures. If you plan to climb primarily ice in very cold conditions, go for the warmth of a plastic boot or a modern well-insulated leather/plastic hybrid. If you plan to climb hard mixed routes where you pull on a special boot/crampon hybrid for each burn, then warmth is pretty much irrelevant. Between these two extremes lies the range of ice/mixed boots.

TRADITIONAL ICE BOOTS

Plastic boots are usually warmer than leather boots, but modern insulated leather boots are surprisingly warm if they start the day dry and are well treated with some sort of leather waterproofing. Even the warmest plastic boot will be cold if the liner isn't dry at the start of the day. Leather boots are often touted as being more comfortable than plastic boots, but note that many ice guides prefer to climb in plastic boots—for their comfort. Some leather boot manufacturers are making hybrid "double leather" boots that are very warm and comfortable, while some of the new plastic boots are lighter and more sensitive than many leather boots. Don't assume a plastic boot is heavier than a leather boot; the old plastic boots were quite heavy, but modern plastic boots often weigh less than warm leather boots. Boot demos at ice fests are a great way to figure out what works. In general, if you live in a very cold climate, go with plastic double boots for the warmth; if you live in Europe or the continental United States, go with leather. Once you've decided what level of warmth you need, start working the different brands for fit and performance.

Performance is specific to climbing terrain. If you plan to frontpoint 2000 feet of 45-degree ice, then you want something that takes the strain off your calf muscles; precision footwork isn't an issue. However, if you plan to delicately dance up 2-inch vertical ice, something much more precise and flexible is required, and warmth and support will be cheerfully sacrificed. In general, the harder the climbing becomes, the lighter and more closely fitted boot you will want. I actually find it less fatiguing to climb steep, hard water ice in a relatively light leather boot that fits my foot very well. A lot of calf pump comes from the heel riding up in the boot, but a precisely fitted leather boot tightens down on your instep much better than a plastic boot and helps prevent heel lift. As ice/mixed climbing becomes more technical, the ability to use your ankles also becomes more important, just as with rock shoes. A whole world of possibilities opens up when you're not limited to using just your frontpoints but can smear and edge on small ice nubbins or any irregularity. Just as light hiking boots changed the way people walk in the mountains, lighter boots are changing the way people climb.

Manufacturers build their leather boots around an "average" model of a foot called a last; the last is literally a plastic model of a foot. For leather boots, various pieces of material are cut and then stitched together using the last as a form, sort of like a papier-mâché wire model. If the last doesn't match your foot, you don't have a hope of getting a good fit. Width, foot volume, the heel pocket, and toe room are all very relevant to the fit; find a manufacturer that uses a last that approximates your foot and you are on the way to a good fit. If you like the performance of a boot model but the fit doesn't quite work, try on several pairs—variations in thread tension, piece cutting, and so on can make two supposedly identical boots fit very differently. A good boot cobbler/boot fitter can also do wonders for fit if you have problem feet.

Plastic boot shells should be nearly identical from pair to pair, but they are commonly built in two-size increments; the outside shell for a size 9 is often the same shell as for a size 10 but with a bulkier liner. Check the markings inside the shell on the plastic and see whether you're buying the small version of a larger-sized shell or the full version; a small version can often pack out and become loose over time. It may be worth getting the next size down "punched" at a good boot-fitting shop to more closely fit your foot. An extra pair of insoles in the boot can also take up a slack space while improving warmth dramatically. There is simply no good reason to have painful feet at day's end.

Women or children with small feet often have less selection available in shops; it may be worth going the mail-order route if you find a boot you love but can't get locally.

I like to wax the leather on my boots and gloves regularly; the factory-supplied treatment is usually good for about only two trips. Just a few coats of water-repellent wax on your boots and leather gloves will keep your feet and hands warm each season.

"Fruit boots" for mixed climbing

Keep your boots in the car on the way to the climb, not in the trunk. If you start with cold boots, your feet will tend to stay cold all day. Starting with warm, dry boots makes life just a bit more pleasant.

MIXED BOOTS

Most mixed climbers want the lightest boot they can find that still has a crampon-compatible sole. Many mixed climbers take this a step further by bolting their crampons directly to a very light boot or even to footwear that is not made specifically for ice climbing. I've seen everything from hockey skates to bike shoes used for this purpose, but manufacturers are picking up on the trend and producing boots designed for this game. The drawback to a mixed-specific boot is that climbs need to be approached in a different set of boots, but since most hard mixed routes don't have much in the way of an approach, this isn't a big deal. If you're already climbing M12, you're probably using boots with bolt-on crampons (known as

"fruit boots" in Canada).

If you don't want to build a fruit boot setup, then single leather boots are definitely the way to go—the lighter the better. Any light, crampon-compatible boot will work; how light is determined by how much time you want to spend actually ice climbing, in which you need a bit of mass to drive a crampon, versus how much time you plan to spend on pure mixed climbing, in which driving crampons into the ice is less relevant. If you don't know the answer to this question, borrow some gear until you figure it out. Modern fruit boots just aren't all that great for most ice routes despite claims to the contrary.

The advantages of an integrated boot/crampon setup become apparent after use, but mainly they are much lighter, they climb with extreme sensitivity, and the heel spur doesn't flex the crampon off the boot. I expect to see traditional ice crampons move toward a more positive fit between crampons and boots in the near future (Charlet Moser's system already has), because a solid connection really improves the crampon's performance.

Building your own fruit boots is surprisingly easy. Any fairly stiff shoe will work okay, but over-the-ankle light boots work better—low-cut shoes tend to come off your feet in radical heel-hooks. Take the laces and insole out, line the crampon up carefully where you want it, and drill at least four holes through both crampon and boot: $1/4$" bolts work well. I usually drill one hole through the boot, mark the crampon with the drill bit in place through the boot, drill the first hole in the crampon, attach the crampon to the boot with a bolt, and then mark the other three holes. This system makes sure you get it right and don't end up drilling a lot of random holes. I initially used T-nuts in the soles, but this actually doesn't work well because most soles are too thin to take a T-nut well. Put the nuts on the crampon side and use lock-washers. The heel spur (an old vertical frontpoint works well) can be bolted directly to a light piece of angle iron bolted to the sole. Some people like to have the heel points and will bolt the rear crampon piece to the boot. If you do use the rear crampon piece, don't count on the underfoot strap to add any rigidity; it usually just breaks after a few pitches due to metal fatigue. Use $1/4$" bolts for the back pieces.

Some people grind the soles off their fruit boots before installing the crampons. This does make them lighter, but be sure that your sole isn't holding the boot together!

CRAMPONS

This is a contentious subject. You can probably learn to climb ice well in any crampon, just as it's possible to climb 5.14 in any decent modern rock shoe. Any crampon for ice climbing should fit securely on your boot and be easy to take on and off with cold fingers. "Step-in" two-piece crampons with a heel lever and front bail are most popular in North America,

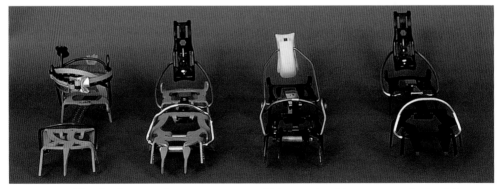

A crampon with a fixed monopoint, two crampons which can take either mono or dual points, a crampon with fixed horizontal dual points

while Europeans generally add a strap to the front bail to help keep the crampon on the boot no matter what. In the past many people used "rigid" crampons for ice climbing, and although these crampons are still sold, most ice climbers now use a two-piece style of crampon.

There are two basic types of crampons: those with fixed dual horizontal frontpoints and those that will accept either one or two vertical frontpoints (the first point or points to hit the ice). Crampons designed for technical terrain will have more aggressive secondary points (the next group to hit the ice after the frontpoints go in), while those designed for mountaineering will have less aggressive frontpoints and likely fewer overall points.

If you're looking for a versatile crampon, get something with two horizontal frontpoints, such as the Black Diamond Sabretooth™ or Charlet Moser Black Ice™. These crampons have good frontpoints and good secondary points and will work well for a variety of conditions. Horizontal frontpoints work far better for most pure ice climbing than vertical frontpoints. Crampons with vertical frontpoints tend to blow out more often, and as soon as you raise your heels at all, with vertical frontpoints they rock out of the ice. The oft-heard refrain of "Keep your heels low!" comes from this very issue. I challenge any climber currently on vertical frontpoints to climb five pitches on a good horizontal frontpoint crampon and feel the difference. Dual frontpoints, either horizontal or vertical, tend to work far better for ice climbing than monos, especially for novices.

Make sure that the secondary points (the first set behind the frontpoints) on any crampon protrude far enough forward to stabilize the frontpoints (the ones that primarily go into the ice). If they don't then the crampon will be much less secure. Also check out how the rest of the points work or are designed to work. Crampon design evolves relatively rapidly; again, try as many pairs as you can to find what works well for you.

I use crampons with one vertical frontpoint (often called a monopoint) for very homogenous, smooth ice that formed slowly. The single monopoint penetrates well in relatively warm ice and just seems to work better in these conditions. This type of "softer" ice often forms in Colorado, Europe, and other relatively warm climates. I also climb most hard mixed routes and compete with monopoint crampons. Granite cracks tend to form vertically, and a mono slots into vertical slots much better. Competition routes tend to feature drilled holes and other small features that a mono fits into a little better. As usual, try lots of crampons in different conditions and ask around about what climbers prefer in your area.

Take your boots with you into a local shop when buying crampons and make sure that the crampons you like will fit your boots; surprisingly, this is not a given! You may have to pound the bails onto your boots to make them fit into the groove, and some boots simply won't work with some bails. A little bit of pounding is okay, but if you really have to smash the bail, then it's going to be a nightmare in the field. Be sure to remove all snow and ice from the groove.

Adjust your crampons carefully; I see few well-adjusted crampons in the field. I like to have most (generally about 1½ inches) of the frontpoints sticking out past the front of the boot for ice climbing and a bit less (1 to 1¼ inches) for alpine or glacier travel. The bail strap connects the front and back halves of the crampon. This, in conjunction with the heel lever, sets the amount of tension on the crampon. If there isn't enough tension between the heel bail and front wire bail, then the crampon will move around as you kick or may even fall off. Most crampons have two "locator" posts on the back half of the crampon to help keep the heel from moving around. When you pull the heel lever up to tighten the crampon, these two posts should pop around the heel and fit tightly. If they are loose, the whole crampon will move around too much. I like to set the length of the crampon with the bail strap and then adjust the heel bail to really crank the crampon down on the boot. A lot of tension helps suck the bail tightly onto the front of the boot, which makes kicking the ice more efficient and guarantees the crampon will stay put.

MIXED CRAMPONS

Mixed-specific crampons need to be super-light and have a radical heel spur. The heel spur makes them nearly useless for walking around (they feel and act like skis on the back of each boot), but a good, solid heel spur is essential for harder mixed climbing. Several companies now make minimalist mixed crampons with shorter sidepoints (long sidepoints tend to make walking feel like you're on stilts in a light mixed boot), a permanent heel spur, and predrilled holes for directly attaching the crampon to the boot. The Charlet Darts™ are about the best of the mixed bunch at the moment for non-bolt-on crampons (they are also good for bolting on); their unique heel tension system holds the spur tightly against the sole of the boot. A direct bolt-on spur is still better, but the Dart system is a good compromise.

Whichever type of crampon you choose, be sure to keep the front- and sidepoints sharp; nothing degrades performance more than dull points, yet most climbers don't keep them half sharp enough.

ROPES

Any ice climbing rope should be labeled as "Dry," meaning it's relatively resistant to absorbing a lot of water. These ropes cost a bit more, but they tend not to turn into frozen cables as quickly. Rope choices bring out strong emotions in climbers: some prefer to climb on one single 9.4mm rope, others are adamant that two "Half" ropes are the choice because they can be clipped in to alternating pieces of protection. Ropes labeled as "Twin" must be clipped in together to every piece of protection, so most ice climbers avoid them. Here are the pros and cons of each system.

Single ropes reduce the clutter at belays and while you are leading and they can be used with a Grigri™ (provided the rope isn't icy and difficult to feed) for those desperately long leads. A single rope is lighter on lead than two half ropes, but if the climbers will be rappelling the route, then either the raps will be limited to half-rope distances or an additional skinny rope must be carried. On pure ice routes, rope drag tends to be relatively minimal because ice creates very little friction, and it's normally possible to place the protection in a fairly straight line. For most pure ice routes I've found one single rope is easier to deal with than two half ropes. If I must rap, I carry an additional very light twin rope in the bottom of my pack and pull it out at the top of the route.

In general, I like to lead traditional (nonbolted) mixed climbs on two ropes certified by the Union Internationale des Associations d'Alpinisme (UIAA) as half ropes. A half rope is designed to be clipped in to alternating pieces of gear. Do not confuse this with twin ropes, which are designed to both be clipped in to each piece of gear. Half ropes are rated to absorb relatively benign falls on a single strand; twin ropes are not. For traditional-style mixed routes with very technical protection, such as thin smears where the gear is primarily rock gear on either side of the smear, I tend to use half ropes because they offer more flexibility and require fewer slings. Traditional mixed climbs also often have sharp edges, loose blocks, and other rope-threatening features; two ropes make me feel safer. Be sure to clip in each rope singly, not both ropes together, to alternating pieces. Clipping both ropes through one carabiner leads to the ropes running through the 'biner at different rates

of speed; this can cut or severely damage the ropes! Two half ropes offer more protection opportunities and lower impact forces in the event of a fall; lower impact forces become important if your gear is less than bomber, a common situation on ice routes. Two half ropes weigh less than a single rope and a second rap rope for long routes. Half ropes are also great for belaying two seconds up at the same time; on long alpine routes attempted with three people, I use half ropes exclusively. Very complicated terrain, such as massive icicles, wild mixed routes, or other "three-dimensional" terrain, is also best climbed with two half ropes.

LENGTH

I prefer 70-meter ropes for ice climbing; the extra length can really speed up a long route and often allows three- or even four-pitch routes to be done in two pitches. Rappelling efficiency is also greatly improved. Creating a good belay is often the slowest part of ice climbing, so reducing the number of belays is faster, and speed generally equals warmth and safety on an ice route. Remember that just because you have the extra length doesn't mean you have to use it; if there's a great belay after 40 meters then by all means take it.

Examine your ropes regularly, preferably after every climbing day. It's surprising how often a second will neatly bisect the core while following a pitch; sooner or later the rope will flick into the path of the swinging tool at exactly the wrong moment. Cut the damaged end off (another argument for starting with a 70-meter rope).

Grivel 360, Black Diamond Turbo screws

ICE SCREWS

First, buy good screws. At the time of this writing I can honestly recommend only the Black Diamond Turbo/Express™ and the Grivel 360™ (I'm sponsored by Black Diamond, but note what good non-BD-sponsored climbers usually climb with.) Any other screw I've tested just doesn't work very well. These two screws start easily and spin in fast thanks to their crank handles. The Grivel fits well into indents thanks to its wire handle, but doesn't rack as well. Another company may come out with a really good screw after this is published, so do the research (magazine articles, what local climbers are using, etc.). It's far better to have 10 good screws than 20 that are hard to place and that were made with the quality control of a Russian submarine (most titanium screws) or that wear out after one route (a surprising number of good-looking screws are junk). I haven't placed a pound-in screw in 10 years. They are relatively weak in most ice, are difficult to remove, shatter the ice during placement, and can't compete with modern screws. See the "Leading Ice" section in Chapter 4, Anchors, Belaying, and Leading, for more information.

HELMETS

I never climb ice without a helmet. This is not so much for large objects or ice falling from above (although a helmet is a plus in that situation) but for deflecting the ice we all knock off on ourselves as we climb. Ice climbing helmets tend to take a lot of abuse. A rock climbing helmet may never see even a mild impact over the course of a season, but ice helmets will take numerous minor impacts on even a short pitch of fresh ice due to overhead cleaning and plunging "dinner plates." For this reason I prefer a "classic" helmet with a thick plastic shell rather than a foam helmet with a thin shell. Try to find one that completely covers your forehead; this is essential for deflecting

debris and will reduce impromptu blood-donation sessions. Make sure that your helmet is Comitée Européen de Normalisation (CEN) or UIAA certified; any nonclimbing-specific helmet is unsuitable for ice climbing. Ice helmets should also be easily adjustable for different hats. I often start the day with a thick hat under my helmet and end it with no hat, so easy adjustment is critical.

HARNESSES

Any decent harness will work well for ice climbing provided that the leg and waist loops will accommodate the amount of clothing you plan to wear. Test this at home. I've seen a few people arrive at the base of an ice route only to discover that their harness won't close over the added insulation of a thick pile jacket and outer layer, which is embarrassing. For mixed routes I tend to wear a light sport-style harness as the needs are fairly similar to a sport climb. On longer routes I like a harness with leg loops that adjust and drop independently of the waist loop; there are times when you want to stay tied in to the waist loop while changing pants or lightening an internal load. Some ice-specific harnesses have openings between the waist strap and padding to attach Ice Clippers™ (see the "Accessories" section). If I could have only one harness, it would definitely be one with adjustable, droppable leg loops and a waist belt that easily adjusts from one base layer to several for cold days. A full-strength haul loop and four gear loops are also useful.

BELAY DEVICES

A good ice belay device needs to work well for belaying and rappelling on a variety of rope diameters, regardless of rope conditions. An ATC-style belay device is the most common for belaying the leader and rappelling. For belaying the second, a European-style plaquette is a very common addition; this allows the leader to eat, drink, and still provide a solid belay to the second. A plaquette is also convenient for bringing up two seconds at the same time

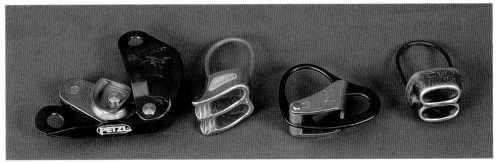

Petzl Gri-Gri, Black Diamond ATC-XP, Petzl Reverso, Black Diamond ATC

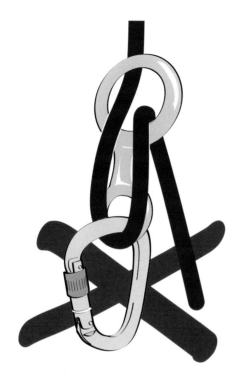

Figure 2. *Belaying with a figure 8 in "sport" mode is not recommended.*

(see "Big Routes: Modern Tactics for Speed and Warmth" in Chapter 3, Basic Ice Climbing). The Petzl Reverso™ combines both functions into one device but has an added advantage in that a plaquette may flip over during use. I've had this happen with skinny ropes on a plaquette, and it's always exciting for the second to note that he basically isn't on belay any more.

Grigris™ can be useful if the rope is dry and ice-free, but they are heavier and tend to increase the impact force on protection. Some climbers will use a Grigri™ to belay the

leader on a long lead with good gear and definitely use one for bolted mixed climbing, but in general Grigris™ aren't an ideal ice belay device. Figure eights are heavy, twist the rope excessively, and have fallen out of favor in recent years (see Figure 2).

All belay devices should be used with a solid locking carabiner, but avoid the complicated "Press the button, twist, pull, etc." style of belay devices. They are nearly impossible to work when you are wearing thick gloves and they tend to ice up very readily. A simple screw mechanism seems to work the best. If a locking carabiner gets stuck, try gently tapping the screw mechanism with one tool or if that fails, warming it up with your hand.

HEADLAMPS

Ice climbing tends to take place during the relatively short days of winter, so a good headlamp is essential. I always throw one of the superlight, small LED headlamps into my ditty bag even when I'm out for a short afternoon; an extra ounce feels great when dark-thirty hits suddenly. For sheer burn time a pure light-emitting diode (LED) headlight is hard to beat, but they often don't throw a beam far enough to allow you to see the ends of your ropes on a rap or help with other routefinding decisions. My preferred headlamp is one with an LED and a good halogen beam in the same housing; the LED lasts forever for close-up work while the halogen makes routefinding a lot easier during the approach and retreat. Make sure that whatever light you buy fits

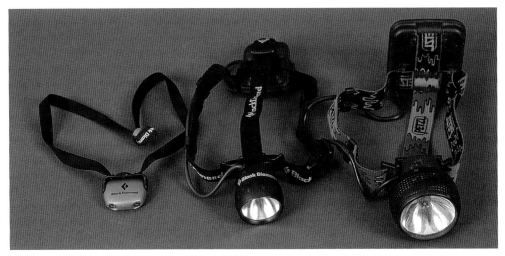

An LED headlamp, LED halogen headlamp, halogen headlamp

well on your helmet; some helmets have lousy attachment systems. Some of the more sophisticated lights on the market offer various settings for the LED and the halogen, and this is a nice feature for saving batteries. Most modern headlamps come with a spare halogen bulb in the housing; this is essential as halogen bulbs don't last that long. LED bulbs generally outlast the life of a headlamp and so aren't replaceable. A headlamp is only as good as the batteries you put in; good alkalines are essential. Rechargeable batteries don't work well in the cold, but some companies make an external rechargeable pack that does work very well.

If you climb in really cold conditions, consider a headlamp with a separate battery pack that you can keep close to your body. Alkaline batteries are nearly useless below –20°C. Alternatively, buy some lithium batteries at a photo store;

they last much longer and are relatively unaffected by cold. They are pricier up front, but the cost per hour of burn time is pretty similar to that of alkalines.

PACKS

Packs are frustrating. Nothing ever seems to work perfectly, so most climbers end up with shelves full of them after a few years of climbing. Any decent ice climbing pack should be large enough to hold all your gear plus a down jacket, lunch, water, spare gloves, and all the other bits that winter climbing requires, plus have a secure system to hold two tools and your crampons. (I've lost three or four tools over the years while unknowingly testing some designer's "improved" system.) The extra stuff involved in winter climbing means winter packs tend to be larger than their summer counter-parts; I like something that's about 50 liters in size. Avoid packs with overly complex suspension systems and lots of doodads. Some so-called ice packs weigh in at over 5 pounds—this is ridiculous. Shoot for something that weighs 3 pounds or less and has a removable waist belt for those times when you're climbing with a harness on. If the pack doesn't have an exterior crampon holder, buy a tough crampon-specific bag that can also hold about a dozen ice screws. Keeping the pointy bits away from your down jacket and other gear will cut down on duct-tape repair.

A harness outfitted with Ice Clippers for screws

ACCESSORIES

Racking ice screws is a real pain; they're hard to get off a floating carabiner with one hand, and if they're not lined up carefully they'll poke holes in your clothing. Some companies make rubber-band systems that allow you to lock one or a couple of carabiners on to your harness in a fixed position; they make removing screws a lot simpler. Black Diamond sells plastic Ice Clippers™ with a wire gate. This type of clip fits onto your harness, is light and simple, and makes removing screws much easier than any other system. Ice Clippers™ also fit through the head on almost any ice tool; just clip the tool in when you're not using it. This system has replaced the traditional ice-tool holster for most climbers, but if your tools won't work with Clippers then get a couple of ice-tool holsters and put them on your harness.

A thermos full of hot soup or sugar-laden tea can offer a real physical and psychological shot of warmth on cold days. If the approach isn't too long, I'll carry a big thermos for everyone to enjoy. On very cold days I use insulated water-bottle sleeves and pour near-boiling water into Nalgene™ bottles. (Get the clear kind; they can take hot liquids better than the opaque variety.) Always use a wide-mouth water bottle; narrow-mouth bottles often fill up with ice quickly. You can break the ice on a wide-mouth Nalgene™ bottle, but a narrow-mouth one will keep your water on the wrong side of a frozen plug. Wrap your warm-water-filled bottle in your down

GEAR MAINTENANCE

The best thing you can do to preserve your gear is to dry it all out every day after you return to the ranch. If you don't spend the time to fully dry it after each trip, screws and crampons will rust, threads will corrode, and boots will start to smell really evil. The evening drying ritual is also a good time to examine your gear for new damage; I've found unexplainable crampon holes in my rope this way more than once. If the relative humidity is low, the gear will dry quickly even in cool temperatures, but if it's humid in the room, you'll need some heat. Be careful not to use too much heat. If you can't hold your hand comfortably on your gear, it's too much heat. Nylon has a very low melting point!

jacket inside your pack (use a good-quality Nalgene™ bottle that won't leak) and it will stay liquid a lot longer plus preheat your jacket, which feels nice at the belay.

Bladder systems such as Camelbaks™ are great for warmer days; the Platypus™ bags can be filled with boiling water in the morning and they retain heat for a surprising amount of time. (Don't put even warm tap water into a Dromedary™ or Camelbak™ bag; it will wreck the valve seal). If the air temperature is warm (near freezing) then a hose is a good addition, especially on the approach, when staying hydrated is essential. On any day below about –5° C (23° F) hoses freeze up, and then you have no way to get at your water.

Eye protection is essential for any outdoor sport, and ice climbing is no exception. A sunny day on an ice climb can be extremely bright. Goggles tend to be too unwieldy, awkward, and prone to fogging up; I prefer some sort of sunglass system in which I can change the lenses based on the day and how scratched they become. Avoid anything close-fitting; they will only fog up. In colder, snowier conditions with spindrift avalanches or large amounts of blowing snow, goggles are essential, but I generally bring them only on long alpine routes.

Sunscreen is the last obvious necessity!

SHOPPING FOR ICE GEAR

If you can, try out ice gear at an ice demo and make your decisions based on a combination of what you like and what trusted friends use. Ice demos often have beat-out ice that could be climbed with a set of steak knives and hobnail boots, so try to test the gear on fresh ice. It's surprising how a quick lap up a fresh bit of ice will change your opinion about what really works!

Magazine reviews can be a good source of information, but I've written enough of them to know they are usually written quickly with less-than-optimum amounts of research. What worked great in Colorado during the magazine's month of testing may be totally inappropriate for Canada in January. Read reviews with an eye toward what you want, not necessarily what the writer felt was important. A good knowledgeable shop is a great resource, and I try to support local shops whenever possible. Spending 5 percent more to shop locally is good for the local economy and climbing scene. Local shops provide an invaluable service for customer support and general knowledge. We've all gone into a local shop for advice on what to buy, climb, or wear, and I think that resource is worth supporting. Mail order can be good for a great price, but if something goes wrong with the gear you've got to ship it back and deal with the hassle. In contrast, a local shop knows you will be around for years and wants to keep a happy customer, so they will work for you.

Used ice gear is often a good buy for those who can recognize and evaluate current brands. If you can't afford the new stuff and don't know the brands intimately, conscript a more knowledgeable friend to review potential deals. Failing that, make sure that replacement parts (especially picks) are still available, and stay well clear of anything more than about five years old. Boots are probably the best buy used if you can find something that fits you and meets your needs; it's easy to see the wear problems. Unless they still have the hang tags in place, used ice screws are almost always a bad buy; even mildly dinged teeth take all the fun out of placing a screw. I avoid used carabiners, harnesses, ropes, and other life-critical gear. Even if it's in a fresh bag, its history is still suspect, and peace of mind is worth a lot when the ice gets interesting.

PICK MAINTENANCE

Picks arrive fresh and optimistic, then we beat the hell out of them! We all know we're not supposed to swing hard when the ice is thin, but then we get totally gripped out of our minds and swing like carpenters anyhow. The result is a pick that looks more useful for tilling the garden than climbing.

Maintenance is about bringing a pick back reasonably close to its factory specifications and performance; tweaking is all about making a pick work for you. Two simple tools are helpful: a good metal flat

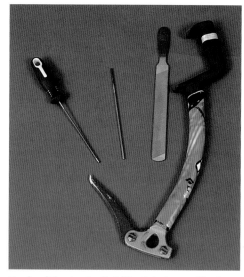

Tools of the trade: flat file, "chainsaw files"

A radically filed pick for better penetration

file and a good round file with the same radius as the teeth on your tool (sometimes called "chainsaw files"). I never use grinders on my picks; I've found that an electric grinder too often destroys the temper of the steel. The only pick I've broken in the last 10 years was one I'd worked on with a grinder. If you do use a grinder, use it very briefly (five seconds or less) and cool the pick with water between grinds.

If you have a vise to hold your tools, use it. I like to sit on a low chair or step. You need to support the tool well because if the pick moves around, you can't file evenly and will end up with a rounded pick.

The first goal is to get the tip "prow" back in business. You'll have to remove enough steel off the tip and sides of the pick so that it looks the same as it did when it came out of the box. Just making it sharp again but leaving the damaged shape isn't good enough. The pick must be filed so that when swung the very tip of the pick hits the ice first; rounded shapes or other weirdness won't work well. This restoration process makes the pick shorter,

but I'll keep using the same pick until I've shortened it by about $^3/_4$ inch. Use firm, smooth strokes to remove the damaged steel, keeping the file working in the same flat plane. If you have one, look at a fresh pick and notice how the angles are clean, not rounded.

After you've got the prow shape of the tip back to original, it's time for the teeth. If you're just taking out minor burrs, you can probably keep the same first tooth. File the underside of the first tooth back to normal with a flat file. If you've really beaten on

Support the tool in this position for best results.

Before: A banged up pick

After: functional once more

the pick, you'll have to flat-file past the first tooth and let the second tooth become the first tooth. Don't try to leave funky little teeth close to the tip; this makes the tip of the tool weaker and will shorten its life span. Use the round file and flat file to buff out any tooth damage; using a flat file to work on teeth leaves stress points that will definitely be weaker.

PICK TWEAKING

Overall pick design has really improved in the last five years, but many of us still like to "tweak" our picks. Tweaking is all about making a pick work for you. I see a lot of pick tweaking that actually harms the performance of the pick; here's how to tweak picks for various desired functions. Note that tweaking voids your warranty and will probably make the pick weaker than stock. Picks are designed with care to be strong, so changing the shape of anything changes the stress structure. If you still want to modify your picks, here's how to do it.

For better-penetrating picks you'll want to remove surface area and volume on the very tip or "prow" of the pick. The more you remove, the better the pick will penetrate. At some point you'll remove too much and it will break easily but penetrate brilliantly. Remove the steel symmetrically so that the pick retains the same basic thickness as the original. Making the end very, very pointed works well for penetration but even a light hit on rock will crumple it like tinfoil. Your budget for new picks may determine how low-profile you want to go. Taper the overall volume of the pick back from the tip smoothly; big "steps" in taper will keep it from penetrating well. Also be sure to keep the cutting edge on top sharp and tapered.

How "sticky" a pick seems is determined primarily by how deep the teeth are, how much bevel is on the teeth, how steep the initial tooth is, and how sharp the cutting edge on top of the pick is. If you look at most picks, you'll see the actual teeth are narrower than the width of the pick; this difference is the amount of "bevel" on the teeth. Slightly beveled teeth dig into the ice better because there is more pressure on each point (think dull crampons versus sharp crampons), but they are also easier to remove because there is less "catching" area on each tooth. A little bevel and moderate teeth stick predictably, penetrate better, and seem to shatter less ice. If you want to make each placement crazy bomber, make the teeth deeper (use the round file to radius the corners) and use no bevel. Unfortunately, this type of pick will often break since it will take huge forces to remove. It's also inefficient to have overly sticky picks; they lead to all sorts of unbalanced antics while you are trying to get the tool out.

If you radically increase the angle of the last tooth, it will be great for thin hooking but also prone to sticking irreparably. This type of pick can break while ice climbing normally because the forces during removal will be very high on a small piece of steel. Most people don't pay enough attention to the cutting surface on top of their picks. This surface also must be maintained for easy removal and kept constant as you modify other elements on your pick.

For mixed climbing I generally keep my pick completely stock, as it came from the shop, except for the angle of the first tooth, being especially careful to make the tip hook extremely sharp and square. A pick filed like this will place tremendous amounts of force on the rock as you hang on it, which will help it hold on even smooth edges. If I have to climb a delicate icicle at the top, I'll also set the tip up for best penetration, but this means the pick will crumple easily if I hit rock. In general, I run two sets of picks: one fairly stock for working on routes and general climbing and one for those desperate redpoints and sick icicles. Very thin cracks sometimes demand a very thin pick, and I'll modify mine to fit into them, but this makes the pick quite weak when torqued in the same crack. One day we'll have picks as thin as knives that will take any degree of abuse, but until then we'll be going through a fair number of picks each season.

SCREWS

It's always a shock to discover that a $50 screw is nearly worthless despite "just gently touching the rock." The best defense for dull screws is to use the appropriate length and be very careful about turning them in if you have any doubts about the depth of the ice. However, if you've done the deed and banged the teeth, it's possible to make a damaged screw work reasonably well. Position the screw securely between two blocks of wood in the jaws of a vise. Now get out the round file you use on your picks and a small oval file with the same curve as the tooth. I keep a good screw on the bench as I work so I can compare the two. File each tooth until it matches the good screw. This is a slow and painstaking business, but it gets easier with practice. Resist the temptation to make the teeth sharper than factory spec; this will just make them weak and they will bend in even normal ice.

CHAPTER 2

Will Gadd on "Power to Burn," Banff National Park, Canada

Dress and Eat for Success

Staying warm, dry, and comfortable while ice climbing is an art; unfortunately, most of the art professors out there must live in relatively warm places, as their words are often ridiculous. Here's how to stay warm and comfortable in any conditions.

There are three fundamental tricks to staying warm in any miserable climate: Stay dry, stay fed, and stay ahead of the game. While this may seem like a boy-scout mantra, it works. Staying dry means keeping your clothes and skin moisture-free. Staying fed means keeping enough calories in your system so that you can keep moving, feel fresh, and continually dry your clothes out. Staying ahead means just that: anticipating what the conditions will be in the next 10 minutes or hour and planning intelligently for them. Let's follow two teams as they each head out ice climbing.

Joe and Susy arrive in the parking lot, jump out of the car, pull on lots of clothes and a set of stylish top and bottom three-layer Gore-Tex™ shells because "it's cold out today!" Then they finish sorting gear and bust a move up the trail. After about 10 minutes they are sweaty but don't want to "stop so soon" to take clothes off, so they continue on, getting sweatier, and finally stop to take some clothes off—but it's too late for Joe and Susy. Their base layers are soaked, their socks are soaked, the inside of their outer layers has condensation on it, and they have just wasted a lot of energy and water cooling their bodies on a cold day—sort of like air conditioning a house in the middle of winter because the furnace is on too high. All of their moisture (which means having to drink more later) will add up to cold feet, cold hands, and general misery later in the day.

Scott and Betty arrive in the parking lot about an hour after Joe and Susy have left and note, "Man, it's cold today!" They sort gear wearing big down jackets and thick hats, get the packs all dialed in, and then, at the last minute, strip off the down jackets and hats and get down to one thin layer of polypro on the top and a layer of polypro and Scholler™ fabric on the bottom, plus superthin gloves and headbands. At first they are a bit chilly, as usual, but after they move for a few minutes, their hands and feet feel warm, but they're not sweating. Because they are wearing very little clothing, they regulate their temperature primarily by their speed of movement; on the flats they move a bit quicker, on the steep hills they slow down to keep from heating up too much. After a while even the thin gloves and headbands go into pant pockets and the shirts are rolled back to expose forearms, further helping to cool their furnaces.

Meanwhile, Joe and Susy's hands are cold. They started the day wearing lots of fleece, full Gore-Tex™ suits, and super-thick "Mega Ice 4000" gloves, all of which filled with sweat in the first 30 minutes of walking. After they stopped and removed some layers, their bodies suddenly became mini-evaporative coolers because of all the moisture next to the skin. The fleece in their gloves is wet also, so as Joe and Susy's bodies shunt blood flow to their cores to dry out all that polypro, cold hands set in. Joe and Susy stop, pull on all their damp fleece and Gore-Tex™ that they had taken off earlier, and find their bodies starting to sweat again, even though their hands still feel cold and clammy. Joe and Susy stop to pull on their backup pair of dry gloves, which they then also sweat out. Scott and Betty march by Joe and Susy at about this point.

After a couple of hours Scott and Betty arrive at the base of their route; both bare some skin and pull on dry polypro shirts, then quickly add another light piece of fleece. Scott adds a Scholler™ soft top; Betty goes for a very thin Gore-Tex™ shell. Both suck back a half liter of water and a large roll filled with sausage and cheese; each already had two gels and a half liter of water on the hike in. Betty wins the ice ax toss, so Scott pulls on his monster down jacket, thick hat, and mitts and zips Betty's down jacket around his legs for extra warmth. He's warm, dry, and comfortable. Betty starts up wearing a pair of very light polypro gloves with an uncoated nylon shell. It takes Betty about 30 minutes to lead the pitch, and just as Scott's is starting to feel a bit of a chill, she yells, "Off!" Betty pulls on her belay mitts, which were clipped to the back of her harness, while Scott quickly stuffs all his warm clothing into the pack and runs up to the belay dressed in less than most people wear to the mall. Betty's is still warm despite wearing very little, but she replaces her light gloves with a fresh set before starting up the next pitch on her "block" because her hands got wet leading the first pitch. Even though Scott feels warm now, he pulls on all the warm clothing again before he begins to feel cold. Neither one will get cold hands or feel more than mildly chilled all day.

Joe and Susy finally get to the base of their route, which is straight across from Scott and Betty's, and note that the "underdressed" team that passed them is already two pitches up and moving well. Joe and Susy add down jackets over their full-body Gore-Tex™ outfits, and Joe heads up because Susy's hands feel cold and she wants to warm them up. Joe climbs in a full suit of Gore-Tex™ over two layers of fleece; he arrives at the belay so steamy he can't see out of his glasses, while Susy's hands and feet are numb. Joe shivers and curses as his sweat runs in icy rivulets down his neck while Susy attempts to follow the pitch with numb hands, which takes a long time and doesn't improve their personal relationship. When Susy finally gets to the belay, Joe realizes he's superhungry and that he hasn't eaten anything since that bowl of cereal four hours earlier. They eat a couple of gels but don't feel much like drinking water because they're cold, so the gel doesn't digest well. They rap a few cold pitches later and note that the underdressed team is relaxing in the sun in the valley bottom drinking tea.

This tale of two climbing parties isn't exaggerated. I see variations of this story all the time in the mountains, even in relatively warm temperatures.

TECHNICAL CLOTHING

Being cold is not a mandatory ice climbing experience; suffering is a failure in planning and systems.

Ice climbing clothing isn't just fashion; it's warmth, safety, and even happiness. Good systems make the difference between being psyched to climb and going home early.

GLOVES

Bring several pairs of dry, light gloves. Most "ice climbing gloves" are too heavy and just get filled with sweat. It's better to bring a pair of mitts for belays and up to four pairs of semi-disposable light gloves for climbing in. Windstopper™ or a very light breathable nylon shell over a thin glove liner seems to work well for most people, even in cold temperatures—again, it's primarily core temperature that determines hand warmth, not the amount of insulation on your hands when you are moving.

The "screaming barfies" are an aptly named experience that occurs when blood flows back into cold hands; the feeling of simultaneously wanting to scream and barf is one of the least pleasant experiences around. If your hands are dry and your core is warm, you won't get screaming barfies. Let your core temperature drop at the belay, wear sweat-soaked (even if thick) gloves at the start of the pitch, and you're almost guaranteed a round with the barfies. If you're prone to getting screaming barfies, review your systems for maintaining core temperature and always having dry gloves; barfies are avoidable. Barfies are also more common early in the season, probably because climbers oversqueeze their tools at the start of the season, which prevents blood from flowing through the fingers. Following all of the points listed above will greatly reduce the problem!

SHELLS

Any shell should be extremely breathable and have a hood; a hood keeps blowing snow out of your inner layers when conditions get miserable and adds a lot of heat retention for cold days. Thick (three-layer) Gore-Tex™ or other heavy, "crunchy," waterproof-breathable shells are suitable only for climbing up really, really wet climbs or for very wet approaches. I haven't worn this type of shell in years. I do wear a light, thin shell made out of the lightest possible Gore-Tex™ fairly often while climbing, especially on wet climbs, but I almost never wear this on the approach. Insulated soft-shell fabrics work very well on my legs, but I haven't had as good luck with them on my upper body; most seem stiff, don't fit well under a harness, don't move well, and may offer too much insulation. I prefer either no upper-body shell if conditions are dry or the very lightest possible Gore-Tex™ shell if conditions are wet.

Scholler™ or other "faced" fabrics are often referred to as "soft shell" fabrics. This type of clothing is evolving rapidly and is increasingly popular for cold-weather climbing. I often wear a Scholler™ top; this resists the occasional icy rivulet, seems windproof enough, and moves well. I have worn only Scholler™ pants for the last five years, but I will sometimes bring a pair of superlight Gore-Tex™ bottoms for digging snow caves, for skiing, or in case it starts raining on the walk out.

HATS AND BALACLAVAS

Yes. I have a full drawer of hats, and I select what to wear each day as carefully as what I bring on the rack. Thin helmet liners, thick hats for hanging out, neck gaiters—I use them all depending on the temperature and forecast. I like to carry a very thin balaclava in the top of my pack; it really helps retain heat, maybe because it covers the neck. Wool hats get wet, don't fit under helmets, and usually fall down over your eyes. Get close-fitting fleece hats instead, in a variety of weights.

GAITERS

Gaiters are another trade-off—sometimes necessary to keep snow out of your boots but total moisture traps for the steam rising out of your boots. My feet get a lot wetter due to condensation when I wear gaiters, but they get wetter still if snow falls into my boots. Unless I'm postholing through wet snow, I like to use just the elasticized cuff of my Scholler™ pants as my gaiter. Some pants have eyelets for a string under your boot to hold the pant down; this is a good system. If I have to wear gaiters, I use light and thin Gore-Tex™ because nothing else breathes as well in my experience.

SOCKS

Good socks aren't cheap, but they can make a huge difference in comfort and do last a long time. I like to wear one thin inner sock and one slightly thicker outer sock; this combination seems to keep my feet drier and help prevent blisters. Bring a spare sock system if your feet sweat a lot and change your socks at the base of the climb.

Kevin Mahoney dressed for a belay session.
Photo © Will Gadd

SURVIVING LONG BELAYS

Long belays require careful core-temperature maintenance even with a big belay jacket and good mitts. For starters, make sure you're fed and dry, then plan ahead to avoid a miserable experience. Muscle motion is the only way to stay warm when the temperature is really cold. If the belay lasts more than about 10 minutes in cold weather, I do standing knee raises, lifting one knee at a time to my chest, followed by 50 arm windmills on each side followed by 20 more leg raises, repeating until I'm truly warm. Squats are good too. The key is to start doing all these exercises while you're still warm or just starting to cool down; it's a lot easier to stay warm than it is to warm up a chilled core. Also try to take the weight off your harness at midroute belays; harnesses constrict blood flow to your feet.

Here are a few "rules" for staying warm and comfortable in the winter.

- It's better to be slightly cold while moving than drenched in sweat. Do your best to avoid sweating on the approach, even if it means being stripped naked and moving slower. Sweat will make your feet and core cold later in the day, and a cold core makes you move slower in the long run. If you sweat a lot no matter how little clothing you wear, bring at least a spare set of synthetic socks and an extra dry shirt.

- Your legs sweat less than your upper body. Many climbers find they can get away with slightly more clothing on their legs than their upper bodies—as long as it's very breathable—and stay drier and warmer with this tactic.

- Your hands and feet will be warm if they are dry and if your core is warm enough. If your hands or feet are wet, then they will be cold unless you're really working hard. But if your core is chilled, no gloves or socks, no matter how massive, will keep them warm.

- Put on all available clothing as soon as you stop someplace where you'll be standing around for a while (belays). Most people put on warm clothes only when they start to cool down; this is too late, just as taking clothing off after 30 minutes of sweating is too late. This is particularly important when you arrive at the base of the climb.

- Layering for ice climbing means having an "aerobic" approach outfit, a "climbing" outfit (generally just a light shell over a thin base layer), and a "stand around" outfit. Too many complicated layers are a pain to take on and off, so get your basic outfits figured out and then add a big down jacket for belays.

- Treat all your outer clothing with a good Dry Water Repellent (DWR); the best is the type you add to a washing machine full of outerwear. Interestingly, the reason that Gore-Tex™ appears to degrade after use is not due to the membrane breaking down (it's extremely durable) but to the DWR losing effectiveness. Once the DWR is "tired," the face fabric absorbs water and the Gore-Tex™ ceases to function as effectively.

- Be careful to keep snow out of gloves, dust off snow accumulations on pants, and just generally be painstakingly careful to reduce the amount of cold snow coming into contact with warm surfaces. I can always tell someone who is experienced at staying dry by how carefully they remove their gloves and store them to stay snow-free.

- Temperatures within a few degrees of freezing are the hardest to stay warm in, especially if it's snowing. The wet snow tends to melt on your clothing and get it wet, but wearing any sort of shell results in a soaked body due to the "warm" temperature. Accept this, bring a spare shirt, and dress as lightly as possible. Very light Gore-Tex™ is often a good choice on wet climbs, on spring climbs, or if you climb in a coastal-influenced area; just

Fueling up with a Yule Log, en route to the climb. Photo © Raphael Slawinski

dress as lightly as possible under it.

■ Remove ear, nose, and other piercings; these conduct cold nicely and will freeze flesh quickly.

■ Wear a hat, balaclava, or scarf in windy conditions to prevent frostbite. I'm partial to a neck gaiter pulled up high on my face, but if the weather is really miserable then only a balaclava will work.

NUTRITION FOR COLD CLIMBING

I often read that the best breakfast for a winter's day out is a bowl of oatmeal with bananas or some such fluff; that's an okay breakfast for a quick run, but for ice climbing I'd add some sausages, a couple of eggs, some hash browns with extra grease, and a big glass of orange juice to wash it all down with. I don't care what the "science" of nutrition says about this; my partners and I climb a lot in cold conditions and we know that it works. It took me many years of trial-and-error eating to realize that fat and protein are my friends in winter; carbohydrates (sugar, bread, gel, anything that's not fat or protein) still form the bulk of my actual calories, but they go on a solid base of fat and protein.

If I've had a really good breakfast then I can go most of the day on a gel every 40 minutes along with plenty of water, but I find my body works better with "real" food at some point during the day. If you're going hard for more than 12 hours, take lessons from the ultrarunners; they all use gel or drink mixes religiously, but definitely take some solid food about every 8 hours—or more often. Some people can go for many hours on pure gel; experiment with what works for you.

Caffeine and nicotine generally aren't helpful for keeping you warm, but caffeine and sugar can help keep you moving well throughout the day, which will help keep you warm. I like sugar-laced strong tea after about 6 hours of movement.

For a long day out I'll generally take the following food and eat it on this schedule:

Dinner the night before: A big pasta dinner with plenty of protein, washed down with plenty of water all evening. I find that having a well-fueled and well-hydrated body at the start of the day often begins the night before.

6:00 A.M. breakfast: "Trucker's Special" or equivalent 2 to 3 hours before I start walking in to the route. If it's a long walk and a big climb, I'll commonly eat more than 1000 calories at the first meal. This might mean four eggs, two pieces of well-buttered toast, a sausage or two, a couple of tortillas, and anything else that looks palatable. If it's a very early start, I'll make a couple of massive egg, sausage, bean, cheese, and salsa burritos to eat on the drive to the climb. I like to have an hour or two to digest before walking in, but since most walks in to ice climbs are not conducted at extreme heart rates, I can walk and digest at the same time.

8:00 A.M.–12:00 P.M.: At least ¼ liter of water per hour and a gel every 45 minutes or so. I like to fill one pocket on my pants with hard candies; they are fun to eat, digest well (simple sugar), and seem to keep my blood sugar relatively level when I'm exercising.

Lunch: Big turkey sandwich and a big peanut butter cookie.

1:00 P.M.–dark: A couple of candy bars or gels every 45 minutes, plus another liter of water.

Back at the car: Another liter or two of water (rehydration is critical; no matter how much you drank, you're probably dehydrated) and the turkey sandwich I left there for just this occasion. This should be eaten immediately; your body absorbs food better immediately after hard exercise.

Dinner: Water and pasta with protein. I'm usually not starving at dinner, and extreme hunger indicates I didn't feed my body carefully all day and am deep in calorie debt. This is damaging and will slow recovery for the festivities the next day.

Snacks: Cheese, sausage, chocolate, nuts, crackers, energy bars, (Clif Bars™ don't freeze as hard as some others), and my personal favorite, Oreos™. Avoid vegetables or fruit—they freeze.

Kim Csizmazia on "Ain't Nobody Here But Us Chickens," Waterfowl Lake Gullies, Banff National Park, Canada

CLIMB ICE!

When I started climbing I never thought I would ice climb—I assumed it was cold and nasty. I would have ignored it completely, but my boyfriend was a fanatic. He prosely-tized as he mock-swung his ice tools. He prayed for cold. Then one day he took me to a Jeff Lowe slide show. There I saw pictures of ice sculpted like blue glass and I became a disciple.

Many women are turned off by the perceived discomfort of ice climbing just as I was. The cold, the danger, and the gear are intimidating. In addition, women often find it uncomfortable to explore and express themselves in a male environment. Ice climbing has been a mostly male club.

Most women are convinced they are going to freeze to death if they go ice climbing because they seem to get cold easier than their male partners. However, as Will said earlier in this chapter, "Being cold is not an unavoidable part of ice climbing, it's a failure in planning and systems." This is especially true for women.

In general, women have more body fat, slower metabolisms, and poorer circulation. I find that I warm up slower and cool down faster than most of my male partners. Having a lower metabolism means there is less heat to dry out base layers and power warmth out to the extremities. This is further complicated by relatively poor circulation. In addition to following all the principles in this chapter, I have three very important rules for dealing with my tendency to get cold. First, I insist on hiking at my own pace. If I start to sweat, I go slower. This is particularly important at the beginning of the day. I have a rule to walk leisurely for the first 20 minutes to one hour. Second, poor circulation means that even the smallest amount of constriction will make an exponential difference in cold hands and feet. For example, thin, loose gloves will be warmer than thick, snug ones. Experiment and dare to go lighter. Third, drink warm water or fluids. I like warm water so that I can drink a significant volume at once. This dries me out and kick-starts my heater. Cold water, on the other hand, extinguishes it.

If you are well hydrated, you will stay warmer, happier, and stronger. Unfortunately, many women find the inconvenience of relieving themselves sufficient enough to stop drinking. I know a very good female ice climber who developed kidney problems one winter as a result of not drinking all day so that she wouldn't have to pee.

Success in the mountains may come down to overcoming this dilemma in all weather conditions and with any combination of partner, from spouse to best female friend to a roped team of impatient men better equipped by nature than you are to make a clean, efficient job of it. I use crotch zips and a Freshette a.k.a. Lady J™. Without it I feel trapped. Be forewarned: Practice makes perfect, but it is worth it. At 4300 meters (medical camp) on Denali, the toilet sits surrounded by hundreds of tents. It is intimidating. At base camp I peed standing next to a middle-aged man. My partner Julie heard him tell his team about it. She said, "He sounded like he was going to cry."

I used to see women out all the time in huge boots stuck full of socks and hand-me-down gear. They struggled up the ice with heels lifting, wearing ridiculous gloves and carrying dinosaur tools all draped with faded Gore-Tex™. No wonder they thought they sucked. Good gear, especially boots, is imperative.

On my first day out I found the stiff boots, teetering crampons, and sticks lashed to my wrists all very awkward. I knew that I could accept and adapt to the awkwardness except for the 2 inches of heel lift in my boots. They were the right size; they just did not fit. At the time I was working at the Black Diamond retail store, so I spent the whole next day trying on boots. Toward the end of the day I found a pair of discontinued, plastic glacier walking boots stuck in a corner of the boot closet. They felt perfect. My heel did not lift and I could completely flex my ankle. The sole was also relatively soft and it had lots of rocker. These are all characteristics that I look for in boots today. The problem with many boots is that the manufacturers do not take into account weight and leverage when they downsize boots. Think of a 175-pound man in size-10 boots compared to a 125-pound woman in size-6 boots that are the same stiffness. Relatively those boots are much stiffer for the woman, who has less weight to power them and less length to lever them. The biggest difference is in the ability to bend your ankle. Your boots should allow you to move; they should not act like casts. The good news is that many boot manufacturers are now thinking of these things and building boots for women.

The social dynamic of women in the climbing world is complex and entangled. Some ask, "Are women less aggressive, less confident, and more affected by risk than men?" Does it matter? I provide the following only as food for thought and encouragement as you pursue your path as a female climber.

When I first started climbing I took a clinic taught by Amy Irvine and Cathy Boleil, two of the best female rock climbers in the United States at the time. I was so intimidated to sign up for the clinic that my boyfriend paid for it. Then he had to force me to go as though I was a kid going to my first day in a new school. The day turned out to be one of the most influential of my entire climbing history. Amy is a great climber, teacher, and feminist. I learned that I should take control of my climbing by becoming self-sufficient. And I learned that the ultimate goal was to lead because in leading lie the heart and essence of climbing. Here, I feel compelled to echo Amy's teaching and also her voice of caution. When she taught that clinic she was still recovering from a broken back as a result of a climbing accident. She urged us all to take the initiative to keep ourselves safe.

This means learning the skills and enduring an apprenticeship, but it also means knowing when to get on the sharp end of the rope.

I have learned since that that day was important for many more reasons. These reasons are well summarized and documented in a National Outdoor Leadership School (NOLS) training journal article by Missy White but can be summed up in two critical points: One, "For many women, learning skills in a single-gender environment or among friends is a key component to learning successes." And two, "Role models are incredibly important to each of us. Seeing someone achieve at a high level who represents our religion, nationality, gender, or racial background inspires us."

As I wrote this, I asked Will what he thought about women and ice climbing. He replied, "I'm all for it. They look better, they smell better, and I get to lead more."

"Interesting," I thought. "I have led as much ice as any other woman on the planet but he still gets to lead more."

This made me think of a story that a teacher in charge of a high-school climbing wall once told me. She said initially the climbing hour was coed, but she found that the boys would climb while the girls mostly stood and watched. She decided to segregate them. The result was that during their time the girls climbed like crazy. The boys, on the other hand, complained of discrimination. They argued that they had not prevented the girls from climbing. Instead, they felt they had been encouraging. I believe they had the best intentions.

In my opinion the above situation is about a fundamental breakdown in communication and understanding between the sexes. Will's statement summed it up for me. He is very supportive and encouraging of my climbing but it is also normal for him to covet every lead. He does this with male and female partners. What he has experienced is that his male partners insist on their share of leads. However, it is a rare woman who will actively take her turn among the boys. It takes a certain kind of assertiveness associated with adjectives like "pushy" and "aggressive" on the part of the woman. I have heard it called the Hillary Clinton Complex. Women respond best to meaningful encouragement from other women, but when it comes to men, they would rather play cheerleader and keep the waters calm. Kudos to all women out there who prefer to storm the seas. You go, Hillary!

— Kim Csizmazia

CHAPTER 3

Jennifer Davis on R & D, Kananaskis, Canadian Rockies

Basic Ice Climbing

Ice climbing offers a unique look into a magical realm, but climbing in winter demands greater attention to some fundamental details than climbing in summer. All the same hazards of summer are present, but in addition it's cold—and the route is guaranteed to fall down at least once a season. As each climber heads up the route, small but potentially lethal missiles release continuously as a natural result of climbing; if the first rule of ice climbing is "never fall on lead," surely the second is that "moving under any route with a climber above is a good way to get hurt." When approaching any ice climb, stop well back or to the side of where any potential debris may be coming down and get geared up there; put your helmet on first— even if there is no one on the route. I've been hit by falling ice at the base of climbs enough to respect this rule carefully.

From your protected stance away from the climb, get your harness, crampons, rope, and other gear organized. It's easier to put your harness on before your crampons (especially if the leg loops don't open). Be sure to put on your crampons early; you have to put them on at some point, so why not do it earlier rather than scrabbling upward another 20 feet? I've seen some humorous to near-fatal sliding falls on the ice below a route; this strikes me as avoidable. Take a good look at the route above where you plan to climb before setting up your belay; if it's midday sunny and there's a big icicle dangling up there, make sure you'll be out of the way if it comes off. Even a softball-size piece of ice falling on your head or shoulder is painful; ice is surprisingly heavy and sharp. Ice climbing demands more "situational awareness" than rock climbing, so continually ask yourself: What can fall down as temperatures change? Is the snow stable? Is the weather changing rapidly? Are you on schedule to do the climb? Answer these questions continuously while you are climbing to stay safe.

If you plan to lead or top-rope the route, the belayer needs to stand safely out of the way of falling ice. If there is more than one person in the party, everybody needs to be securely out of the way of falling ice. It's not poor form to knock ice off when climbing; "cleaning" is a natural and often essential process. If you do have to cross under climbers on a route, ask them to hold still for a minute, cross, and then tell them that you are clear. Waiting until things seem clear and then sprinting past works some of the time, but not all the time. Many ice areas have some degree of "tourist" traffic; politely explain the situation to them if they try to stand under the climber and watch.

If you are climbing and dislodge a piece with a funky trajectory, yell "Ice!" However, repeatedly yelling "Ice!" in a crowded climbing scene is annoying and eventually reduces the effectiveness of the warning, sort of like crying wolf—reserve your yells for people who may not have noticed you in the area or for really large ice explosions. If there are already climbers on the route you're approaching, decide at a safe distance whether you can climb to the side of them safely or not. If you can't then find another route. Starting up below another party is a great way to find out how good you are at patching up facial lacerations or worse. Ice can move a surprising distance laterally as it falls and also bounce unpredictably as it hits the ground. Better to be well out of the way and safe at all times. I often see inexperienced ice climbers blithely walk up to a route with climbers on it, only to get beaned and aggravated at the climbers on the route; the fault lies with the newcomers, not the climbers on route.

Early season ice: icicles and air

Ice climbing is best learned on a top-rope in a relatively benign environment. In the clinics I teach I try to set up at least three or four top-ropes and get everyone to climb each rope a few times. If you can run 10 laps on a top-rope and play with placements and movement, you'll be much better off than going out and struggling up two pitches in 8 hours on lead. Even a short piece of steep ice can teach a tremendous amount if you run 20 laps on it, plus you'll stay warm, have fun, and greatly increase your knowledge base.

ICE FORMATION: UNDERSTANDING THE MEDIUM

Understanding where to climb means understanding how the ice formed. Only rarely does ice form in nice, neat, uniform layers such as those a Zamboni™ ice tractor lays down on an ice rink—if this were the case the whole sport would be a lot less interesting! Normally ice forms in fits and starts. It melts and freezes, forms in the middle of snowstorms and over old snow, and creates icicles and bulges—all at different temperatures and with different results. All climbs start as "young ice" and progress to "mature ice" before degenerating. Let's run through the ice life cycle.

YOUNG EARLY-CYCLE ICE

Let's start with the perfect ice climb, where a small rivulet seeps out of the ground at the top of a 100-foot vertical wall. During the first cold snap in the fall, ice starts forming in small sheets and patches on the margins of the flowing water. At first this ice will not be well bonded to the rock, but with continued cold temperatures the water freezes hard and the new ice attaches very solidly to the rock. On a microscopic level, rock is extremely featured; this is why bugs can climb across "smooth" rock with ease. Ice fills all these little indentations and protuberances, creating a bond seemingly as strong as crazy glue. Without a good bond the ice is only supporting itself, like stacking logs against the wall—not a very strong situation. The ice/rock bond is also strong in a tensile or "pull" form; like a weld, it will hold very heavy "pull" forces but not bend. This is why pillars are so interesting to climb. Once the ice and rock are frozen together, this bond is capable of supporting the massive weight of free-hanging stalactites weighing thousands of tons, and it's usually the main reason ice climbs stay standing.

The ice of an early season climb will be most organized at the top and increasingly random farther down the climb. In very cold temperatures on steeper routes many icicles will form, and the climb will look

Typical early-season ice. Vertical icicles are difficult.

almost hairy or like a chandelier. The ideal ice-forming temperatures are about –10 to –1°C (14 to 30°F); very cold temperatures will make a lot of ice quickly, but the individual ice features won't connect well until the water has a chance to cement all the icicles together. The most uniform and pleasant ice forms slowly at relatively warm temperatures. Lower-angled ice generally forms quicker and relatively smoother than higher-angled frozen waterfalls.

In consistently cold (just below freezing) but not arctic temperatures, ice tends to form more uniformly, in sheets, with each new sheet bonding well with the sheet below it. Once there are patches of ice down the length of the climb, the ice starts to fill in the gaps between features, greatly increasing the solidity of the ice. On early season routes, the icicles have air space between them, although they are usually more connected at the bottom where the water was dripping back onto the wall or at the top where the water was dripping from. Often a group of icicles will defend a small piece of very good ice at their base.

One-swing "wonder ice" is often found in new ice that formed at very even temperatures with relatively low volumes of water. If the climb has very little water feeding it (but still has some), the pillars or other features that are forming are likely very delicate. Many early season climbs get trashed by climbers breaking off the formative ice. This is selfish because the climb may never recover.

If relatively warm spring water is flowing out of the ground and then immediately over the top of the climb, the last few feet are often very hollow and not well attached; special care must be taken not to knock it all down. It's often safer to retreat off a good V-thread well below the top of this sort of climb than it is to gun it for the trees at the top. Those last few feet of wet, dirty moss and rock can be a real nightmare.

Wet ice is often more plastic and easy to get a good stick in but also relatively weak because its bonds haven't yet solidified into true ice. Be careful climbing wet ice and be suspicious of putting screws into it.

MID-CYCLE ICE

Water begins the ice cycle by flowing and freezing next to the rock, but eventually it gets shunted around as ice forms, disrupting the flow of the water and pushing it off into new channels much like a river in a wide gravel riverbed. The places where the water is shunted and slows down tend to build up into relatively solid platforms of ice; this is the best place for a screw or a tool. If the total flow volume is low, the ice will be relatively dense—even if it's thin. Ice that forms in corners or grooves will have a lot of rock to bond with, tending to create very solid ice. Small overhangs work exactly like the roof on your house: ice drips off in icicles, creating "bead curtains" that eventually fill in until the curtain is solid ice.

Often the freezing water will form "ice tubes," basically ice that looks like a pipe cut in half lengthwise and stuck to the wall. These ice tubes come in all sizes, from too small to hold a pick to many feet across. The outside of these tubes, like any convex

This ice is starting to fill in.

ice, will fracture easily if hit with a pick, but the sides closest to the rock will often be very good because they are supported on two sides. These tubes frequently form beside each other and then gradually fill in as the season progresses; the grooves between them often have the best ice and offer stemming opportunities.

Higher flow volumes tend to create really nasty chandeliered ice until the ice has a chance to fill in. Higher flow volumes on steep walls also tend to create ice with water in mist form; this "spray ice" has more air in it, which makes it less stable and less strong, but also less prone to fracturing with an ice tool. Spray ice forms a lot of the more interesting ice climbs out there. In spots where the ice forms first, more ice will tend to keep forming; the old ice will cool the water, and the air temperature will freeze it rapidly. If water is still running quickly, the ice won't form there.

If there are any small edges or ledges on the rock, the ice will also tend to form there, then drape off the feature. These features are called "ice eyebrows," and on very thin climbs they may be the only solid place to get a tool or ice screw placement. Picture water running off the roof of your house; usually there is a small, solid "ice dam" on the lip of the roof with many icicles hanging below it. This process of building ice dams is what creates the always engaging "ice roof."

MATURE ICE

If a water supply is continuous, ice will continue to form. Larger volumes of water will cause ice to form in spray patterns on the sides and at the bottom of the main flow; eventually the spraying water will freeze high enough on the sides to cover the top of the main flow, creating a tube. On many frozen waterfalls fed by small or large creeks, there will be a hollow core in the middle of the ice flow for part of or even, rarely, the whole season. This doesn't mean the ice climb is automatically unstable, but care must be taken not to fall into the middle of the tube! On these climbs the tube will usually block at some point,

pushing the water out onto the surface.

A mature ice climb will keep forming in new ways if fed water continuously; the paths of flowing water will invariably freeze up, redirecting the water in new directions. I've learned a lot about how vertical ice forms by watching mountain creeks. They almost always "overflow" the first ice of the season, creating new layers in new places.

You may have noticed that ice that is wet one day will be dry the next and later in the week wet again. An arctic front can turn a well-consolidated, mature ice climb into an early season climb again in just a few short days. In general, the best ice has the most consistent temperature. This can be a small microclimate, such as that found in the shade behind a curtain, or a larger microclimate, such as a climb stuck way back in the depths of an icy-cold chimney.

DEGENERATING ICE

All ice climbs are guaranteed to fall down at least once a season, but most ice climbs don't fall down dramatically as the temperature warms; instead, they start to melt on the surface and less-supported features such as long icicles and thin curtains fall off first, then the overall mass of ice gradually decreases. If there is a lot of ice (10 feet wide and 3 feet thick), the ice will resist even very warm temperatures during the day, just as a large block of ice will resist melting for much longer than will a bunch of ice cubes. (Alpine ice climbs may even resist a summer's worth of warmth.) If the temperature drops below freezing at night, even large features will remain solid. However, if

This ice has started to degenerate from sun and high temperatures.

This ice has water behind it and is separating from the rock.

the ice is thin and the temperature well above freezing, meltwater will get behind the ice, breaking the ice/rock bond and making smears and other features very unstable. If the ice is a foot thick and water is running behind it, it still may be safe to climb short sections, but anytime that water is running behind ice and you can see that the ice is not attached to the rock at any point, it's probably time to go rock climbing.

Sun is especially damaging to the surface of ice. "Sun-bleached ice" is white and often has large, loosely bonded crystals. Refrozen sun-bleached ice can be great fun to climb as it accepts tools readily, but realize that it is often worthless for ice screws. If the surface hasn't refrozen, then it often has the consistency of a very thick Slurpee™, and it's easy to rip one or both tools through it. Foot placements spread the weight out over a larger area, but they also tend to fall apart at surprising moments.

Rain and ice climbing are a bad combination; if it's raining, I don't go ice climbing. Even if the rain is cold, it is still much warmer than the ice. Picture pouring warm water down the rock: it eats at the ice/rock bond and often gets behind even large formations and weakens them much faster than a hot day will. I have seen entire climbs completely decompose in a few days of rain at $+3°C$ ($37°F$), while similar climbs will resist many days of even $+10°C$ ($50°F$) heat—especially if the temperature drops to freezing at night.

If the supply of water ends but temperatures remain cold, the ice will start to dry out. What happens when you leave an ice cube in your freezer for a very long time? It becomes increasingly aerated and brittle and loses mass. Many early season climbs that form as a result of the freeze/thaw cycle of melting snow at the top of cliffs will be so dry and brittle later in the season that they are unclimbable. The ice separates off the rock, loses mass, and finally disappears. Wind accelerates this process if temperatures are cold, which makes me think that ice climbs sublimate just as a snow pack does. "Subliminated ice" is often not well bonded to the rock and will make bonging sounds while climbed. This is scary and can be dangerous, so try to figure out why the ice is still standing. I've climbed routes where I honestly can't understand the physics of the ice staying attached. On one route I rapped down the hollow pitch and kicked it; it all fell down. I have less enthusiasm for climbing ice in these conditions now!

SPECIAL FEATURES AND WEIRD ICE

Dinner plates describe any situation in which you hit the ice with your pick and a piece of ice detaches in a rough circle around your pick. Dinner plates can range in size from a few inches to a few feet in diameter, but the root cause is that the top layers of ice are delaminating from the lower layers. I think dinner plates are primarily caused by differences in temperature between the top surface of the ice and the inner surfaces. Very cold days often produce spectacular dinner plates, but so do warm days after long cold periods. Ice that has been consistently very cold for many days is often very, very solid, but warm up the top layer and it's hell to climb. Ice expands and contracts with temperature, just like cement. (Frozen water actually takes up more volume than liquid water.) When the surface layer of ice expands or contracts at a different rate than the subsurface ice, the surface ice will become unstable and prone to dinner plating.

Onion skins usually form when spray lands on the top of a snow ledge or spray cones with a fresh mantle of snow; as the spray lands on the snow and freezes, it creates a shell crust. Later, as more water or spray lands in the same spot, proper ice will form, often several inches thick. Onion skins can be very dangerous; on several occasions I've pulled up onto a large, sloping ledge in the middle of a pitch, stood up on seemingly solid ice, and had it all collapse. Several accidents have been attributed to this type of event. Generally, onion skins sound hollow as you crampon

Cauliflower ice

up them; tread lightly, or try to find a place where the "skin" is very thick and well attached to the general ice flow. Be sure to place a screw before getting on an onion skin; delaminating onion skins are one of the common causes of surprise lead falls. Never place a screw in an onion skin. You can usually feel the screw punch through the top layer into the snow or hollow space under it, so pick another spot.

Cauliflower ice means any ice that forms in really weird shapes, almost always on areas that either are currently being sprayed by falling water or have been in the past. Spraying water can form truly horrendous ice features that combine onion skins, aerated spray ice, and other funkiness into dangerous structures that defy all rational explanation as to why they don't just fall down and break like a stack of china. Often the ice will form in shapes more reminiscent of an opened artichoke than a cauliflower, with upward-sweeping "petals" ranging in size from flattened grapefruits to minivans. The only way to climb many "spray cones" is to break off the vertical ice petals and get at the good ice below. Curtain Call, in the Canadian Rockies, is notorious for producing bad spray cone ice. Until the ice encases the water on the freestanding top pillar, the water is free to fall about 200 feet and blow all over the place on the first pitch—the results are frightening! Often a big snowstorm will further complicate the picture by filling in the gaps between the petals, and then an onion skin will form over the whole mess and the process will start again.

Spray cones are one of the most technical, intriguing, and difficult challenges an ice climber will encounter. Often solid ice is in the middle of a spray cone; dig until you can get a solid placement. Be careful of standing on top of the petals; they are often weak and break suddenly. Better to break them off and stand on the stubs. It may be easier to climb very delicate spray cones with your hands, using the features as rock holds. However, this is far less secure than digging through the petals to find solid placements.

BASIC CRAMPON SKILLS

Crampons initially feel awkward on most people's feet; they tend to catch unpredictably, tear the hell out of pant legs, and sometimes puncture one's calves. The first thing I have new ice climbers do in my clinics is just learn to walk around in their crampons on the flat. Most issues get sorted out pretty quickly. Here are a few tips for moving around at the base of ice climbs or on low-angle ice.

- Place the crampon flat on the ice with all points contacting it whenever possible (wearing a flexible boot helps). Slam it down hard when the ice is at a low angle; the points really have to dig in to properly engage. On low-angle ice, crampons don't "edge" like a rock shoe. The French call walking up low-angle ice with all the points touching the ice "flat-foot" technique; all this means is keeping all the crampon points flat on the ice. (See Figure 3)

- Be careful not to catch any of the points on the ground or on your pants. Falling down after catching a point is comical on flat ground, but it can be deadly on steeper ground. Slow down and think about each foot placement anytime there is a risk of a long plummet. Eventually crampon use will become instinctive, but they are awkward at first.

- Low-angle ice is dangerous. It's easy to start sliding if you misstep and fall down. Be smooth and aware of what's below you at all times! If you're walking around on a big low-angle ice ledge over a 30-foot drop, you're basically soloing—put a rope on!

- Be more careful than normal when descending. The heel points on crampons do not work like a boot heel on dirt. If you can't get all the points of the crampon flat on the ice, turn around and frontpoint down the ice.

Figure 3. *Flat-footing (or French technique) involves keeping you boot soles parallel to the surface. Keep feet slightly farther apart than normal to avoid snagging a crampon.*

BASIC ICE MOVEMENT

Rock climbing often feels more natural at first for novices than ice climbing due to all the extra ice gear, but with time and good basic technique the ice gear will truly start to feel like an extension of the climber's central nervous system. This state of gear/body integration begins when ice climbing stops feeling like a vertical battle and becomes a vertical dance.

OVERALL STRATEGY

The best line up a frozen waterfall is seldom straight up the middle. Before starting up any ice climb, stop and have a good, appraising look at it. A minute spent planning the attack can be worth hours spent trying to figure out what to do once in motion. In general, go for the most well formed, consolidated ice. This ice is usually found in all the places discussed above: corners, the space between two tubes, places where the ice has formed and consolidated into sheets, and so on. Avoid icy curtains, ice that formed in the middle of the flow during the last arctic front, and sun-bleached sections. I like to stand at the bottom and mentally plan my line through all these features first. It's surprisingly easy to mentally lose track of where you are on a climb. You can save a lot of time if you remember to step right around that curtain or move left to avoid the sun-bleached nightmare you saw from the ground. Don't forget that it's always possible to climb down a few feet or move laterally instead of continuing to beat your way straight up.

Three components need to work together when climbing ice: the swing, the kick, and the system you use to move with between placements. Here's how each component works individually and as a system.

THE SWING

Learning to swing an ice tool well can take years—or 10 minutes. The idea is to get the pick to penetrate the ice and stick well. If you can do this without bashing your knuckles and with a minimum number of swings, you're probably doing it right. The rest is refinement and what keeps ice climbing interesting year after year. The following swing is the basis for all the others, so learn it well.

1. Keep your shoulder, elbow, wrist, and the head of the tool all in one plane through each swing. Another way of saying this is that all these parts should line up vertically if someone were looking straight at you. If your elbow or hand is out to

Photo 3-1

the side, then the tool won't swing straight into the ice.

2. Start with your elbow level with your shoulder. On steeper ice it may have to be a little above your shoulder.

3. Let your hand and arm relax so the ice tool falls back. If you're wearing a full pack, the head of the tool would bounce off it. (See Photo 3-1)

4. Keeping your elbow high, fire your triceps muscle (that's the one on the back of your arm). This starts your arm moving toward the ice. Do not use your wrist at this point in the swing; in fact, your wrist should be almost totally relaxed and the tool should still be fairly far back. (See Photo 3-2)

5. Just before your forearm reaches vertical start a very fast wrist-flick.

6. Flick your wrist like casting a fishing rod, keeping the head of the tool, your wrist, your hand, and your elbow all in a good clean line.

7. The head of the tool will accelerate

Photo 3-2

Photo 3-3

very quickly, while your arm is almost totally stationary.

8. If you did the above correctly, the pick will hit the ice cleanly, with force, and your knuckles will be about an inch away from the ice. Your arm should be nearly straight as the tool connects with the ice. (See Photo 3-3)

Problems and Solutions

■ Many novices keep their elbows too low, which results in an ineffectual "pecking"

swing that will not penetrate the ice. Raise the elbow. (See Photo 3-4)

■ Not relaxing the wrist before the flick causes a very "wooden" looking swing; the wrist flick truly generates at least 70 percent of the power of the swing. Without this flick, climbers will also hit their knuckles. (The wrist is clenched so it can't snap the head of the ice tool forward, which makes the knuckles hit first.) Remember to relax the wrist so that the tool naturally falls back. The farther back the head of the tool starts its rotation, the

Photo 3-4. Bad position: Elbow too low

Photo 3-5. Bad position: Not flicking the wrist properly

more power the swing will have. (See Photo 3-5)

- Be sure to watch as much of the swing as possible. It's like trying to hit a tennis ball or a baseball; if you don't watch it all the way, you'll miss the spot you swung for. I can immediately tell a good climber from a newer climber by how close each swing comes to the placement they are building. I find sunglasses or clear lenses help me swing more accurately (provided they don't fog up).

- Swing with your fingers relatively relaxed on the grip but holding the shape of the tool fairly securely. Most tools will swing better and faster if you hold your pointer finger and thumb in an oval shape with the other fingers fairly open. This positioning allows the tool to rotate cleanly forward as you snap your wrist, yet the oval shape of your fingers guides it carefully toward the ice. Squeezing the tool hard prevents rotating your hand, clenches your wrist, and leads to cold hands. Most novices get cold fingers at first because they are squeezing the tool like a rattlesnake's head, which cuts off circulation to the fingers and prevents this natural rotation in the hand.

- If you swing with your elbow out to the side of your shoulder like a chicken wing, then the swing will have no power and no accuracy unless you're a very accomplished climber. Keeping everything lined up as described earlier until you develop a good swing is critical. You can swing out to the side if you keep

Photo 3-6. The chicken wing swing

your tool, hand, and elbow aligned carefully. If your wrist is curved inward, it's almost impossible to swing well. (See Photo 3-6)

- If you are using leashes be certain they are set up as described earlier in the Gear section: your little finger should be just below the shaft/spike joint. Improper hand position is often at the root of swing problems.

- Different tools swing differently; adapt your swing to the tool you're climbing with.

Good Placement versus Bad Placement

A good placement, or "stick," is one that will hold securely even if both feet blow simultaneously. A bad stick is anything less than this. It still may be very useful or even the only thing available, but without at least one bomber placement the game is getting much more serious and needs to be rethought carefully. The sound of the tool as it sticks into the ice provides your first clue. If the tool made a good clean *thunk* sound and feels like it's planted into concrete, it's probably solid. If it's not good, pull it out and get a good stick. It truly is your primary belay at all times when ice climbing. Good placements may take a half-dozen swings to build or even more in really atrocious ice. Make them good. If you don't think the placement is bomber, resist the temptation to just move anyhow—make it good. With practice you'll come to intuitively know the difference between a good stick and a poor stick, but this takes time.

Test Your Placements

If you have any doubt at all about the quality of a placement, give it a hard jerk by snapping your arm down violently. If it's a bad hook or something, it will shear or wobble—reset it. If the stick passes this test, then you know it will hold a fair amount of weight if you keep even pressure on it as you move. Twisting the shaft of an ice tool or changing the direction of the pull is a bad idea; keep it smooth.

Hitting on a concave surface may fracture the ice.

Where to Swing (and Kick)

If you watch a good ice climber in motion you will see her repeatedly look up, pick a spot (sometimes by touching her pick to the spot), and then precisely swing at that spot as many times as it takes to get a good placement. Ice looks relatively similar to a novice ice climber, but knowing where to swing can save tremendous amounts of time and energy. Any convex (the angles on the outside of a mixing bowl) ice will fracture far more than concave ice. Convex ice is found on bulges, the front or most rounded side of pillars, overhangs, and other features where the ice changes angle relatively quickly. Hitting these spots will generally cause the ice to fracture into "dinner plates" (see the "Special Features and Weird Ice" section), plates of ice anywhere from a few inches to a few feet in diameter. Aim for the back of small corners, the back of small ledges, the back of grooves, or anywhere the ice has formed solidly and is supported around the area you plan to hit.

Use your helmet—rather than soft tissue—to block ice debris while cleaning.

Small corners and convex features support the ice and reduce fracturing.

If the ice breaks into dinner plates when hit, it may leave some very nice ice under it. Some climbs require repeated, aggressive swings to remove the top 2 or 3 inches of poor ice to get at the good stuff underneath. Don't rush this process; just accept that you will be doing some heavy-duty construction work on the pitch and work it out methodically. If you swing and break ice off over your head, put your helmet forward and let it, not your face, take the impact. Many climbers have a tendency to turn their heads sideways and back to "miss" the ice; usually the falling ice then just hits them in the nose or cheek. Your helmet is protection, so use it to let the ice bounce off or over. A quick ducking motion seems to work well. You want to watch the pick enter the ice for accuracy, but often it will break small pieces off. Don't be shy, just snap your head forward and let the helmet do its job.

When climbing up under an icicle-loaded feature, try to take the icicles down in small pieces off to the side, then climb up and through the spot you've cleared.

Classic "beat-out" ice: good for hooks

Icicles can cause serious facial injuries when they break; clearing them out before engaging the obstacle is critical. If you can't get totally out to the side, move as much to the side as you can, get a bomber placement, and take the icicles down in relatively small pieces by gently breaking off the bottom, then the middle, then the top. This is an essential skill for climbing ice safely.

If you're climbing ice that has already been climbed, even by only one other person, use the old pick holes and foot placements. Climbs that have seen a lot of traffic are referred to as "beat out," and they may have a ladderlike series of fist-size or larger holes all the way up. If you try to swing at the fresh ice between these holes the ice will usually just shatter; instead, swing into the back of the old holes using a bit more downward wrist flick to seat the tip of your tool in the good ice in the very back of the hole. If the holes are deep, the best option is to "hook" them by putting your tool in the hole and pulling down. Usually the hole will be lower in the back of the pocket than in the front, so as long as you don't pull directly out, the placement is very secure. Play with this on a top-rope so you get a good feel for it before heading up on lead! As with all placements, test the hook by pulling down hard while your other tool is still well planted.

THE KICK

Good ice climbers place their feet as carefully as their tools. To do this you must look at your feet before placing them;

Keep your leg relatively parallel to the ice; most of the power comes from below the knee.

Note that the secondary points are well-engaged.

blindly kicking at the ice is a common error. On a relatively smooth sheet of ice, look down and kick it hard! This shatters the top layer of the ice, leaving a more solid "pocket." Look down where you kicked, and then kick again in the same spot. After a couple of good hard kicks, you should get a very solid foot placement. Unless the ice is very wet or warm, you will probably have to kick two or three times to make a good foot placement. Your feet should always

have more weight on them than your arms, so take the time to build good footholds and you will relax your arms more, knowing that your feet are solid.

Once your foot is well connected to the ice, keep it in the same position as much as possible while moving your other foot or tools. If you raise your heel to make a bit longer reach with your tool, the toe of your boot will lever the frontpoints out. "Keep your heels low!" is an oft-repeated comment

This climber's feet are too high: the toes of the boots are forcing the front points out.

features you would use if you were rock climbing, and then use them with your crampons. Choose a small bump, divot, or other feature that you might want to use as a partial foothold, and then kick your crampon in just above it. This spot will generally be supported by the feature, which you can then use as a partial foothold in addition to your frontpoints. If the feature is delicate, kick lightly but repeatedly to build a good hold without fracturing the feature off.

PUTTING IT TOGETHER: TRACKING

Most novice ice climbers tend to place both tools side by side for each upward movement. This method is slow, often insecure, and very tiring. "Tracking" is a more efficient alternative method for climbing ice of any angle. This style of ice climbing is both faster and more secure, which means more fun and less fatigue on steeper ice. Less fatigue means greater security because climbing doesn't generally become difficult until the climber gets tired. Practice this or any new ice technique on top-rope first; you will learn a lot more without fear.

This is how to do it.

1. Place your right tool over your head in the ice. Relax and hang straight-armed from this tool.
2. Move both feet up to about mid-shin level, using small steps. Place your feet so they and your upper tool are in a triangle; one foot should be to the left of the "fall line" from your

at ice climbing areas for this reason. Raising your heels too much causes the frontpoints to blow out. Keep your heels low; this takes less muscle and keeps the frontpoints in the ice.

On rock you can often just slap your foot on and then smear, letting your ankle flex and torque over a fairly wide range of motions, but these small motions will tend to blow a crampon off the ice quite quickly.

Most ice is far more featured than it appears from a distance. Identify the

Photo 3-7. The upper tool and feet should form a triangle for stability.

Photo 3-8. Placing the upper tool

high tool, the other to the right. This is a very stable position. (See Photo 3-7) If both your feet are off to one side of your tool, you'll tend to "barn door."

3. Look up and pick a spot for your next tool placement. Planning this movement in advance keeps you from hanging with bent arms while searching the ice for the next placement. The spot should be about a foot higher than your other tool and at shoulder width or narrower away from it. Keep your high arm straight.

4. Loosen your lower tool by pulling up on the grip like it's a pump handle. The top of your pick is designed to cut the ice and make it easier to

Photo 3-9. This climber is "barn-dooring" off.

remove the pick. You don't totally remove it, just loosen it.

5. Pull up on the high tool using the lower tool for balance and additional "push." Rotate your body slightly as you pull up until your arm is either fully "locked off" or bent almost 90 degrees; rotating your body slightly while pushing through the movement with your feet takes a lot less energy than keeping your body exactly square to the ice. (See Photo 3-8)

6. Remove the lower tool and swing it at the spot you already eyeballed. Make this placement solid; the idea is to make fewer but very solid placements. Hang straight-armed from the high tool and move your feet up and under the new high placement. Relax.

7. Repeat to the top!

Problems and Solutions

Most climbers spend far too much time on bent arms. The only time your arms

Photo 3-10

Photo 3-11

should bend is when pulling up to swing at your predetermined spot. If you're locked off and looking for a place to swing, you're wasting energy.

- Keep your feet at roughly the same horizontal level; letting one foot lag behind and below usually makes the frontpoints blow out as you stand up. (See Photo 3-9)
- As soon as your tool is in the ice, relax your upper hand slightly rather than clenching the tool in a death grip.

Photo 3-12. Gently *tap the tool with your palm.*

Relaxed hands also stay warmer.

- Stuck tools are common for novices. Most of the time a stuck tool is at or above head-height; if it were lower you could just pull up hard on the handle and rip it out. This is another reason to place your tools with decent vertical separation; they will not get stuck if you have some vertical distance between them! If the tool is stuck solidly, place the other one higher, pull up, and rip the lower tool out by pulling up sharply on the shaft like a pump handle. (See Photos 3-10/11) If you can't use this tactic, do your best to lever the tool out. Some climbers bang the heel of their hand on the head of the tool. (See Photo 3-12) This works well, but I see some climbers doing this every other move because they are climbing with their tools at the same level. Climb with your tools properly staggered and this won't be a problem!
- If you're having trouble remembering this movement sequence, think of moving one tool, then both feet, then the other tool, then both feet. "One tool, two feet."
- If you are using leashes, let the leash do the work. Consciously relax your hand until the leash is holding all the downward weight and your fingers are only controlling the tool lightly so it doesn't spin sideways suddenly.

PULLING BULGES

My first memorable battle of the bulge came 15 years ago. I had just led my first full pitch of vertical ice, 100 feet of Dali-esque chandeliers that blew up like crystal in the −6°C (21°F) temps. My face was bleeding from shrapnel, my hands were locked into a death cramp on my straight-shafted tools, and my calves were pumped well past their safe operating pressure. All that stood between me and complete safety was the transition from 90-degree ice to a hockey rink.

Too pumped to place a screw and rationalizing that the top of the climb was less than three feet away, I threw my tools at the ice in a spasm of lactic-acid miscontrol and pulled a world-class WWF grovel to get my waist almost level with the

Photo 3-14

top of the climb. Success was in the bag until both my feet blew, one tool ripped, and I was left searching for the friction coefficient of a frozen mitten and an ice tool. There had to be a better way.

Today I still regard bulges with suspicion, but they have become considerably easier with better gear and an evolved technique. First, bent-shaft tools make clearing any bulge easier. There is really no reason, other than bad credit, to climb with a straight-shafted tool. Leather or modern soft plastic boots allow for superior ankle articulation, which is also key for surviving the battle of the bulge.

In general, treat a bulge as you would a slab climb; try to keep the force straight

Photo 3-13

Photo 3-15

down on your feet rather than hugging the rock. Hugging the rock or ice tends to make your feet blow off.

There are three broad concepts to remember for bulges (and ice climbing in general): keep your arms straight and your legs bent, take small steps, and never place your tools side by side.

Here's the system.

1. First, place a screw below the bulge. Bulges are sneaky and deserve your respect. Plant one tool about a foot below the lip; the ice on bulges is almost always bad right at the lip, but place a tool as close to it as you can without serving yourself a nasty dinner plate of ice. (See Photo 3-13)

2. Loosen your lower tool, hike your feet up, and stand up. Then release the lower tool and place it over the lip at a comfortable reach. Keep your hand away from the ice and snap your tool in a fast arc, without moving your arm too much. Don't try to reach too far, just get a good tool in over the lip. Hang straight-armed off your upper tool—many people make the mistake of promptly locking off on the upper tool, which wastes energy and puts your body too close to the ice to see your feet. If your body is too close to the ice, you can't effectively kick your crampons. (See Photo 3-14)

3. Bring your feet up in small steps, about six inches at a time, until they are just below your waist. Loosen your lower tool, stand up, and place your upper tool at a comfortable distance past the lower tool. Relax. If you're spending more than a few seconds locked off on your arm you're doing this wrong.

4. Keep your heels level with or below your frontpoints. As soon as your heels come up more than about 20 degrees from horizontal (i.e., the back of your foot is higher than the front-points) your crampons will blow out.

5. Using small steps and keeping your upper arm straight, walk your feet up to the top of the bulge. If you try to do this with your arms locked off and your chest close to the ice, your feet will blow. Keep at least a foot or

two between your body and the ice at all times! (See Photo 3-15)

6. Resist the urge to go fast. Focus on keeping your weight over your feet, using your tools for balance.

Problems and Solutions

- If you keep your arms bent and your legs straight, your feet will blow, resulting in the infamous fish flop. (See Photo 3-16) Keep your legs bent as you move up on straight arms and it will be a lot easier to kick accurately too.

- Make sure that you stand up slowly and place your crampons firmly after

Photo 3-17

clearing the bulge. If you don't feel secure then go ahead and "crawl," keeping a solid tool placement as a self-belay for each move until you truly feel established on the top.

Photo 3-16. Keep your legs bent and heels low to avoid the embarrassing fishflop.

TRAVERSING

It's almost always better to move gradually sideways and upward than to traverse horizontally. Traversing straight across an ice flow demands multiple placements for every foot of horizontal progress, and traverses are difficult to protect well for

Photo 3-18

Photo 3-19. Resist the temptation to swing too far out to the side.

both the leader and the second. Sometimes traversing is unavoidable—here's how to do it well.

1. Reach out to the side about two feet and get a good placement. Attempting to reach too far is a waste of time and makes it harder to swing accurately. (See Photo 3-17)

2. Use small, secure steps to move under the new placement. Small, smooth footsteps are safer than trying to cross your feet unless the ice is dead simple. (See Photo 3-18)

3. Remove the second tool and place it about 16 inches to the side of the first one. Don't place it too close or it may shatter the ice, blowing out both tools. (See Photo 3-19)

4. Make another placement to the side and move under it, remove your other tool, and place it into the hole you just used. This means making less distance between placements, but it's ultimately easier. Note that the climber's hand, arm, and shoulder are all aligned even though he is swinging

out to the side.

5. Sometimes it's okay to get tricky. If you have leashless tools, matching them speeds up the whole process; with leashed tools you can cross one over the other. Be careful when prying the "back" tool out not to pop the other one out as well!

MORE TRICKS AND TECHNIQUES

A good ice climber will move smoothly upward and not fall. A very good ice climber will make the process look easy and relaxed as though she were a 5.11 rock climber on a pleasant juggy 5.8. This level of skill generally takes a few seasons to develop, but if you master the basic swing, kick, and tracking movement pattern you're well on your way. The following are some more advanced moves that may also help.

Hooking

Hooking means using any ice feature you find without swinging hard into the ice. Beat-out climbs such as those found at popular practice areas often end up with a series of incut "dog dishes" all the way up them. Beat-out climbs work perfectly for practicing hooking and can be raced up on a top-rope, but they still require skill to lead because the placements aren't as secure; the pick is just hooked, not stuck into the ice. Sometimes a hook will be so deep that only the very back teeth of the ice tool will be touching; this type of hook is very stable. On delicate climbs, hooking small natural features or gently tapping a small hole and

"Hooking" between icicles

then hooking it is the only way to ascend without breaking the feature.

Judge each potential hook first by how solid the ice is around it. If it's a dog dish in solid ice, it will hold anything, as long as you keep the force straight down. If the ice seems solid, note how deep the hook is; a very shallow hook isn't worth much, but if the ice is solid it may work well. I will often gently tap the hook to set the tip of my pick into it. Swinging harder and harder into hooks won't make them any better, in fact they may just get deeper and deeper until you wind up with the shaft of your tool on the outer lip of the hook. This can still be solid, but it feels insecure.

I tend to treat hooks very much like drytool problems: if you can keep the tool

in exactly the same position with exactly
the same load, then it will hold, but pull up,
out, or sideways too much and it may slide
off whatever it's hooked on or in. If the ice
around the hook is unconsolidated, trust it
less. It's always a good idea to give a hook a
good, firm pull straight down to test its
solidity. See Chapter 7 for ideas on how to
improve hooking skills.

Stemming

A good stem is a beautiful thing. Stemming
takes the weight off your arms, makes it

*Many climbers forget about the outside points
of their crampons.*

easy to place protection, and allows a restful
stance on which to regroup before the next
section's attack. I often watch climbers pass
perfect stems because they are too con-
sumed by the action to look around. Good
stems can be found between two small
pillars, two large cauliflowers, or often
between the ice and the rock at its side.

Backstepping

If you can find a solid foothold, then a
backstep will work well for a long reach up
or sideways. Be sure the foot is solid; all
your weight will be on it as you reach, and
if that one foot blows, the force will really
shock-load your arm. If the foothold is
large, you can even get the whole side rail

*A few gentle taps and a "hook" work
best here.*

of your crampon on it, but backstepping will also work well with your foot turned sideways about 45 degrees.

ICE GRADES

A typical ice route will be described in the following way: Polar Circus, 700M, V, WI 5. Polar Circus is the name of the route, 700M is the amount of climbing (not straight vertical distance) from the bottom to the top, the roman numeral V is an "alpine" grade and gives an overall length/commitment rating, and the WI stands for Water Ice and gives a guess at how hard the hardest pure ice pitch is. WI ratings mix the technical "grade," or how hard the route would be on a top-rope, with the "head" grade, or how hard it is to get good gear. The mix is complicated and always changing based on conditions, the leader, the second, the temperature, the gear carried, the distance from a road, and whether Aquarius is rising or falling. Seriously, ice ratings mirror the nature of ice climbing, which is unpredictable.

WI GRADES

WI 1: Solid, thick, low-angle ice that would be easy to climb with one ice tool and 10-point (no frontpoint) crampons.

WI 2: A rambling pitch of low-angle ice; only very surefooted dogs would make it up. There are probably more accidents on grade 2 ice than any other. Climbers often don't bother with a rope or gear, but it's surprising how quickly one can accelerate toward the ground on low-angle ice. A rope is a good idea and always essential for novices.

WI 3: The start of really technical climbing; most climbers will want a rope. May have short steps of near-vertical ice (up to a body length) and longer stretches of 60-degree ice.

WI 4: A short bit of vertical ice or a longer pitch of 75- to 80-degree ice. Most novices will make it up on a top-rope without problems, but leading is serious.

WI 5: A long pitch of solid, vertical ice or a short step of vertical but really funky ice. Retreat from anywhere on the pitch would still be possible most of the time, but finding reliable screws and good belays may be difficult.

WI 6: Overhanging mushrooms with bad gear, very thin vertical ice with bad gear, or anything that freaks the leader out totally. Free-hanging daggers, very strenuous ice roofs, or any climbing that seems a lot harder than the consensus grade 5 climbs. Only very experienced, fit climbers will be solid leading at this rating, and even the best climbers will find good reason to retreat occasionally at this rating. Roughly equivalent to 5.9 or easy 5.10 climbing with poor gear and bad rock.

WI 7: Semi-mythical; harder than grade 6, usually with a high publicity coefficient. Most grade 7 routes seem to become grade 6 on the second ascent.

WI 8: Only claimed a few times on pure water ice; very overhanging, with very bad gear and very bad ice, requiring a serious bad-ass to climb it. Alternatively, a very overhanging glacial serac can definitely be equivalent to an M8 in sheer strength, but with very good screws.

Many route descriptions also have an "R" or "X." For example, a 50-meter pitch of 2-inch-thick, less-than-vertical ice is relatively easy to climb if it's well formed but will accept little or no ice protection. This may warrant an R or even X addition. A very thin pillar that flexes while climbed also deserves an X. Most WI 6 routes are automatically R or X.

If the above seems a bit vague and perhaps mildly sarcastic, well, it's because I've yet to really figure the ratings out despite climbing several thousand routes. Take a good look at the route. If it seems like you can climb it safely, then go for it. If it looks silly dangerous and you're not up for that, then don't. Ice routes are usually easier to judge from below than rock routes are, which is both a plus in that you can see what you're getting into and a minus in that you can see what you're getting into.

ALPINE GRADES

Most ice routes also receive an alpine or overall commitment rating. This grade tells you more about the danger level of the climb and its reputation locally.

I: A route you would do after work or during a long lunch. No significant hazard, easy access, and fast descent.

II: A short route close to the road; a fit party could do this in a short morning.

III: As with ice ratings, this is where things get more serious. Some sort of approach, usually multipitch (or one dangerous pitch), and requiring at least a solid half-day.

IV: A longer route in a remote setting, demanding more alpine travel and climbing skills. Or a very difficult, complicated shorter climb.

V: A full-day outing for a competent party in difficult terrain.

VI: Usually a multiday outing on difficult terrain, often involving significant risk. Grade VI routes will seldom be repeated, as they require good conditions and a strong, experienced team with strong motivation.

VII: A route of Himalayan stature and reputation; will generally go years without getting a repeat after the first ascent, and often involves at least one death despite relatively low traffic.

M GRADES

Mixed, for routes with both ice and rock, or "M," grades are less standard from area to area and around the world than ice ratings are, which leads to a lot of confusion. The introduction of shoes with bolted-on crampons and heel spurs has added to the confusion, as it's now possible to rest hanging upside down like a bat. Most M climbs feature relatively decent bolted or rock protection, unless they have an R or X in the rating. Many classic M routes have significant hazard in the form of a large icicle at the end, and the ice climbing on these features may be very difficult compared to classic ice ratings. Here's my take on the current state of M grades, related to rock grade for simplicity. Remember that this comparison assumes technical proficiency at both grades; a solid M10 climber may not have a prayer on a mid-5.12 and vice versa—the skills don't readily transfer.

M5: Roughly equivalent technically to WI 5.

M6: Technically equivalent to WI 6, but well protected and fun.

M7: 5.9–5.10.

M8: Hard 5.10 or easy 5.11.

M9: Hard 5.11 or easy 5.12.

M10: Mid-5.12.

M11: Hard 5.12.

M12: 5.13 depending on gear, conditions, publicity and so on.

BIG ROUTES: MODERN TACTICS FOR SPEED AND WARMTH

Many multiday ice climbs can be done in a day if you're fast. The first ascent of Polar Circus took a week; a fast modern party can comfortably climb it car-to-car in 8 hours. Just because a climb has historically taken a certain amount of time does not mean it will take that much time with modern gear, systems, and tactics.

"Going fast" is a relative idea, which depends on your experience level, objectives, and fitness. Going fast does not mean sprinting along with your heart hammering as though a grizzly is chasing you up the hillside. Going fast means moving efficiently, safely, and continuously at a speed that will produce the best results for the team. Here are some tricks I've learned over the years to complete big (whatever you define as big) routes in a day or less.

The less weight you carry, the faster you will move—if you're competent to cover the terrain with the amount of gear and clothing you're carrying. For example, if you bring eight ice screws up a multipitch vertical climb, you had better be comfortable basically soloing between belays. It may be faster to bring 14 ice screws. Shivering at belays because the day is colder than you expected when you left your down jacket in the car will be slower and less fun. Minimizing gear to maximize speed is an endlessly fascinating skill, perfected only with sufficient failures. Failures are good; they teach us what we need to do differently if we truly analyze what went wrong instead of focusing on the lack of success.

Plan the day in the comfort of your house and get all the gear ready the night before. Organize which car to take, where to park, what gear you will need, who will lead the first block, and how you will get off. This means that when you pull up to the parking lot your packs are thoroughly organized with the rack in the leader's pack, the ropes in the second's pack, and so on. If you're sorting this stuff out at the car when you're cold and not really awake yet, it will take a lot longer than if you had done it the night before.

Start the approach slowly, especially if the day will be a long one. Most climbers sprint for the first 15 minutes, then have to slow down or stop. If your body can't produce enough energy aerobically (at the same rate as you're expending energy), it will go anaerobic and use stored energy instead; when this happens it takes a long time to come out of the anaerobic debt and feel good again. I often go out with climbers who attempt to hammer hard for the first half hour. If I stay with them, I can actually listen to their breathing, watch their heart rates climb, and then see them go anaerobic and have to slow down to a fraction of their early pace until they recover. Usually I just let them jam ahead; it's hard to rein your ego in and do this, but I know I'll go faster overall if I go slower at the start. After about 20 minutes I usually find Mr. Speedy on the side of the trail saying something like, "I just have to catch my breath for a minute." This is the point where they start losing time. When you feel like you have to catch your breath, you're going too hard and will ultimately go slower as the day wears on. I don't know of any formal research on this subject, but I'm convinced that an hour spent moving too fast early in the day will add at least 2 hours to the total time of the day. If you can't comfortably talk as you hike or ski, you're going too fast. Really.

Continue to go slow, especially if the day will be a long one, and eat regularly—but don't stop to rest. This means eating on the move (gels in the pockets), drinking on the move (either with a bladder or an accessible water bottle), and resting only when there's nothing else you can do. As the team arrives at the base of the climb, the leader pulls the rack out, the second is flaking the ropes, and the whole transition from hiking to climbing takes 10 minutes or less. Most climbers waste about 30 minutes at the base of the climb; this is the time it should take to climb

Belaying two seconds at once can be faster with a plaquette or Reverso.

the first pitch. The packs should be organized so that the helmets are on top, followed by climbing clothing, followed by harnesses, followed by gear.

The leader stops at the first belay and puts the second (or two seconds if there are three climbers) on belay with a plaquette or Petzl Reverso™. This system allows him to suck back some water and a gel while safely belaying. The second is ready to climb when the rope goes tight—pack on, boots tight, chomping at the bit. Now it's time to go hard; the second should follow most pitches in one-quarter or less of the time it took the leader to get up it. The second should start reasonably fast, then pick up the speed until arriving at the belay breathing hard (see the "On-Ice Training" section in Chapter 11, Training for Winter Climbing, for how to climb fast). The second clips in to the power point, flips the leader's nicely organized rope stack over onto his rope, puts the leader on belay, and he goes. This transition should take 5 minutes or less, but most climbers take about 15 to 20 minutes to complete it. Note that the same person leads the second pitch as the first; this is called "block leading," and it keeps both climbers warmer and moving faster.

In traditional climbing the climbers "swing leads," or take turns leading: Joe does the first pitch, Betty the second, Joe the third. In block leading one person leads two or more pitches in a row, then the other climber leads two or more, repeat to the top. Block leading is critical for moving fast, but it also makes ice climbing a lot more pleasant because both climbers tend to stay warmer. There's nothing worse than leading a pitch, belaying a slow second up, and then belaying the same second for an hour on a hard lead. It makes a lot more sense for the second to blast up to the leader, arrive warm, put the leader on belay (who is still warm but rested), and repeat until there's a short pitch or walking section where it's good to switch.

Three people can move faster on some long routes than two. For example, the third climber can set the V-threads at the belays for faster rapping on the descent. (A team of two can do this also, but if the second is putting in V-threads, he is probably not really paying attention to the belay.) On long routes it's often faster to have one fresh leader for each block of pitches. If you're climbing with three people, usually both seconds can safely climb side by side at the same time if the leader is using an autolock device such as a plaquette or Petzl Reverso™. (The Reverso™ is preferred because it can't flip over unintentionally.) If the seconds can't safely climb side by side due to limited ice, the route probably isn't a good choice for three people. Some climbers will bring up two seconds in a line, but this is dangerous as the top climber continuously bombards the lower one with ice.

Safety when moving light and fast often lies in correctly analyzing how in control of the time you are and realizing when you are losing control of time. If conditions are bad and it takes three times longer to reach a climb, that's okay, but this fact does not change the other time constraints of the day—the route will still take eight hours, and it will still get dark at the same time. If I think it's going to take six hours to get up a route and two hours to get down, I like to have a few hours in reserve. If it's four o'clock in the afternoon with three pitches left and it gets dark at six, I'll bail if I can't safely descend the climb in the dark. The basic concept of climbing fast and light is moving fast and light, then bailing if it looks like moving fast enough to complete the climb in the time allotted is no longer possible. On some routes you can climb all of it in the dark if need be, so a "day" may be 36 hours; on others where navigation is more complicated, it makes sense to start in the dark and be prepared to finish in the dark. Be aware of when it actually gets light enough to navigate efficiently to the climb; hours may be spent wandering around in the dark, which means you might as well have slept in two more hours.

DANGEROUS TACTICS

The following are common but definitely less-safe systems for moving on ice.

On easy terrain with a lot of steps to catch falling ice. it may be possible to climb simultaneously, or "simulclimb," if both climbers feel very confident about not falling. Simulclimbing just means that the leader goes along placing really good gear at regular intervals until the rope goes tight on the second, who then goes along taking the gear out as the leader continues to climb. This is a great system for covering large amounts of relatively easy terrain, but it depends on the competency of both climbers. If falling ice from the leader will rattle all the way down onto the second, then don't simulclimb. Be sure you always have at least three good pieces of gear between the leader and second anytime you're using a rope. (If you can't get good gear then unrope; at least that way only one person dies if someone falls.) Understand that if the second falls, the force will most likely yank the leader off, who will likely take a bad fall. It's safer and probably faster to belay in pitches if the two climbers aren't both very competent or in situations

in which any ice that the leader knocks off will fall all the way to the second. Keep the rope between climbers relatively snug when moving; a big loop of loose rope may get stuck or create a much longer and more violent fall if someone does peel. If you have any doubt at all about the security of the leader or the second, stop and belay traditionally. Simulclimbing is used only with partners who have complete trust in each other's judgment.

One popular but largely untested trick for simulclimbing is to put a Petzl Tiblock™ on an ice screw or other bomber piece with a locking carabiner; if the second falls, the Tiblock™ may engage and stop the rope from pulling the leader off. Petzl does not recommend this system; if you use it you're playing with fire, but it may offer more security for simulclimbing. It obviously does nothing if the leader falls off. If you're contemplating using this system, be sure to rig it so that the carabiner, not the Tiblock™, takes the force if the leader falls.

Solo climbing is the often overlooked reality of sending larger routes fast. There are a lot of pro and con arguments for soloing, but anyone who has unexpectedly fallen off can relate to how fast "total security" can morph into air whistling by the ears. However, many experienced climbers often solo the short "easy" steps below the "real" climbing. Unless you have a few thousand pitches under your belt and a lot of experience in the mountains, soloing is probably a bad idea. However, if a party of three has to move under seracs on easy terrain then soloing is probably safer.

CHAPTER 4

Scott Semple heading up Curtain Call, Canadian Rockies. (Photo © Will Gadd)

Anchors, Belaying, and Leading

This book assumes a basic familiarity with belay systems and anchors; if you don't have this knowledge then take a good course.

The main requirements for setting up a belay system, whether top-rope or multipitch, are the same. The first requirement is that the belay anchor must safely hold any force the climbers can generate and then some. The second is that the climbers must stay attached to the anchor and to the climb. The third is that the belayer must be able to hold a falling climber. If any one of these systems fails, the result will be dangerous at best.

"Protection" is anything put into the ice or rock to hold a fall or direct the rope. An "anchor" is a system composed of pieces of protection linked together to belay off or through. Slings and/or cord connect pieces of protection to form an anchor. The point at which the equalized pieces of protection come together is called the "focal point."

The focal point is where the climbers clip in to the anchor.

BELAYING

The biggest difference between belaying on rock and belaying on ice is that the friction of the system may be much lower while ice climbing. Icy ropes, cold hands, and a near-frictionless surface all combine to make proper belay technique especially important. I like belay devices shaped like plates or tubes, such as the Black Diamond ATC™, Trango Jaws™, Petzl Reverso™, or similar equipment. Grigris™ may not work well on icy ropes, and the moving parts may fill up with ice. Figure eights are heavy and not suitable for belaying with in general; use a belay-plate/tube device.

Good communication is often difficult while ice climbing; the belayer and climber should work out their communication system before starting up the climb. Always err on the side of caution if communication is compromised or if you're not sure what's happening. If you think the climber is going to reach a top-rope anchor and then break it down and walk off but you can't quite hear what he is saying, keep him on belay until you are positive about what's happening. There's nothing worse than hearing "Take!" from a climber who is no longer on belay.

I like to start each pitch by taking a quick look at my partner's harness and knot; my own knot, belay device, and harness; and the belay. I've caught several potentially lethal errors with this check. The belayer should start with "On belay!" or "I got ya!" The climber should then get established on the ice, say "Climbing!" and the belayer should give a quick "Yep, give her!" before either the climber or the belayer takes the climber's rope out of the focal point on multipitch routes or leaves the ground while top-roping. The point here is not what words are used but that both people understand clearly what's going on and stick to a communication plan.

If the top-roped climber wants the belayer to take the tension out of the rope and hold his weight, then he should say "Take!" "Block" is also increasingly common and means the same thing. If the rope is loose on the climber, then he should say "Up rope!" "Tension" is a less-used word but still common; it means "Keep the rope really tight because I'm scared or tired!" "Slack" means to give the climber a little looser rope. "Falling" means just that and is generally used on lead climbs but is also useful for top-roping.

Always belay off the belay loop if the harness has one; don't clip the carabiner through the leg loops and waist belt if there is a belay loop (see Figure 4). If there is no belay loop then definitely clip the leg loops and waist belt, but any modern harness ought to have a belay loop. The belay loop allows the carabiner to "float" and naturally orient itself in the strongest position in the event of a high load. A carabiner that is "fixed" on your leg and waist loops may be cross-loaded and much weaker.

Especially if the climber weighs a lot more than the belayer, anchor him: if the climber falls, a light unanchored belayer will slide like a hockey puck on ice.

Don't stand way out in front of a climb to belay a leader; you'll get sucked toward the

Wrong . . . Belay close, not far, from the bottom of the climb.

climb and the leader will hit the ground. I anchor the belayer a lot more on ice climbs than I do when rock climbing. In general, anchor the belayer safely off to the side of the climbs well out of the way of any potential falling ice.

TOP-ROPING ANCHORS

Be extra careful when moving around at the top of ice climbs; it's surprisingly easy to trip, and once a climber loses his points on even low-angled ice the trip off the edge can be fast. An extra minute or two rigging a quick belay is worth the time. I often carry two or three 20-foot pieces of 1-inch webbing for setting up top-rope sessions. There are lighter materials out there, but 1-inch webbing is resilient and cheap and inspires confidence. Five or six locking carabiners are also useful.

The most common top-rope anchors are trees. If the tree is alive and at least 8 inches in diameter, then I'll trust it, but I usually back up all top-rope anchors with an ice screw or a backup tree. However, many normally solid trees at the top of ice climbs are in wet soil and may be rotten; a good friend of mine fell 80 feet at Vail when a 6-inch tree ripped out. The tree was rotten, but as none of the trees had leaves this wasn't readily apparent. Quickly slinging a nearby tree or firing in a bomber ice screw as a backup doesn't take much time, and over the years my paranoia about anchor systems has saved my life more than once. Better to be laughed at for an overly secure anchor than to watch a friend go the distance.

The belay loop should be used for belaying and rappelling, so that it loads the carabiner correctly.

When tying in, thread the rope through the waist belt and leg loops.

Avoid stuffing a carabiner through the waist belt and leg loops, as this can lead to the carabiner being loaded incorrectly.

Figure 4. Arrangement of belay device off belay loops.

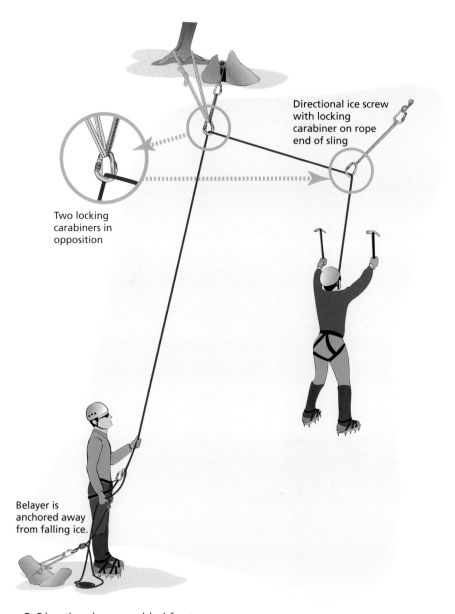

Directional ice screw with locking carabiner on rope end of sling

Two locking carabiners in opposition

Belayer is anchored away from falling ice.

Figure 5. Directional screw added for top-rope

Top-rope anchors may be in place for hours and see a lot of continuous weight. Be aware that ice screws will slowly melt out under pressure. If the weather is cold and the screws are in the shade, then ice screws will last days, but if the screws are in direct sun or the air is warm, screws can become worthless in as little as 20 minutes of hang time. Three equalized ice screws in cold, solid ice are bombproof, but always cover them with snow if they aren't in the shade, and check them after every lap if you have any doubts at all. I have often pulled screws out by hand that were in the sun for as little as half an hour. A lot of the sun's infrared and ultraviolet rays can still make it through thin cloud cover (the same reason we often need sunglasses on a cloudy day). On some days this light may have enough power to heat up the ice screws and loosen them; cover them with snow on any day that seems bright enough for sunglasses, and check the screws regularly.

If the anchor is off to the side of the climb, a "directional" screw or tree at the lip will keep the climber from swinging violently to the side (see Figure 5). Use a quickdraw and two locking carabiners on the directional screw; a nonlocking carabiner can easily unclip as the rope flips around. If the direction is so far off to the side that a failure would lead to a really horrendous swing, then it's really an anchor and should meet the requirements of a belay anchor.

Although it might seem obvious, I've seen two accidents from climbers running the rope straight through the belay sling (see Figure 6)—don't do this! It's okay to run the rap rope through a sling for rapping where the rope is held in place for the duration of the rap, but a loaded top-rope

Figure 6. Never lower or toprope with the rope running directly through a sling, the rope will cut the sling immediately.

running on nylon will cut it very quickly. Always use two opposed carabiners on the focal point, preferably lockers. One locking carabiner is not enough because the gate can easily open. Two non-locking opposed are better than one locker.

LEADING ICE

The first rule of leading ice is "Don't fall." I've been climbing ice for over 20 years and never fallen on an ice screw. Leading an ice climb is not sport climbing or even trad climbing; if your frontpoints catch on the way down, then a badly mangled ankle is a best-case scenario. If I don't honestly feel very confident about leading a pitch without falling (even after starting it), I retreat. Practice for leading ice and placing screws on a snug top-rope. A few days spent running laps on a top-rope will teach even an accomplished climber a lot about security, movement, and ice physics. Leading ice is often more like soloing than normal rock climbing; assuming that a climber could find good ice every 3 meters, the leader would still need to carry 24 screws—six for the two belays and 18 for the 60 meters of climbing. Placing all these screws would take the better part of an afternoon, so most climbers place far fewer.

The second rule is that all belays must be absolutely solid, even if the leader takes a factor-two fall straight onto the belay. The third rule is that the belayer must be protected from friendly fire as the leader sends dozens of potentially damaging missiles down the route. If you follow these three rules religiously you're well on your way to a safe ice climbing career.

PLACING ICE PROTECTION

Placing good ice protection mixes art, science, and educated guesswork. Get the mix right and an ice screw will hold a very violent fall (up to 8,000 pounds of force); get it wrong and watch the screw literally melt out under its own weight. The hard data and research behind the information in this section came primarily from Chris Harmston/Black Diamond and Craig Luebben. Most of their research used Black Diamond or similar tube-style screws with high-relief threads. Apply these theories only to modern screws with high-relief threads.

Twelve to 14 good ice screws should be enough to get you up most any normal route. That's four to six for belays, and eight for the climbing. I'll adjust the mix some for very thin or very fat routes, but my rack is generally composed of one 22cm (for V-threads), seven 19cm, four 16cm, and one 13cm screw. Screws are strongest when placed to the hanger in good ice; tied-off screws are always weaker (see Figure 7a), so use the correct screw length for best results.

The length of the screw is far less important than the quality of the ice. (Research suggests that in solid ice even very short screws can be as strong as long screws.) Many climbers buy all long screws on the theory that long screws are always stronger; this strategy ignores the fact that many of the best placements on ice climbs will not be in the thickest but most protected and best-formed ice, which may be thinner.

Put in good screws before difficult sections like bulges or other terrain that might result in that one-in-a-thousand fall. I always like to have enough gear to keep from hitting a ledge or the ground, which means more screws low on a pitch and fewer high (this is also related to impact forces, which are highest close to the belay). Regardless of the terrain, I put in my first screw no more than three meters above the belay; this avoids factor-two falls onto the belay.

Ice screws generally fail in the following manner: First the ice near the hanger cracks and breaks as the force is applied, then the screw starts bending until the outer portion of the tube is in line with the load. Eventually the tube breaks, the hanger comes off (rare), or the threads rip through the ice. In good ice with a high-quality screw, most of the holding power of a screw comes from its threads, not the mechanical "picket" effect of the tube in the ice. Think about how much harder it is to pull a screw directly out of wood than a nail; the holding power is in the threads. There's been a lot of debate in recent years about positive (hanger lower than the tip of the screw) versus negative (hanger higher than the tip) placement angle, so here's an outline of the physics.

Research to date shows that screws placed with a negative, or "hanger high," angle are, all other factors being equal, significantly weaker (see Figure 7c). Given that most of a screw's holding power comes from the threads—with a modern high-relief thread

screw—it makes sense in general to place the screw with the "hanger low" (positive angle) and more in line with the expected load. I place at least 90 percent of my screws slightly hanger low. This orients the threads more in line with the load and reduces the shearing effect on the tube as ice breaks out around the head under load. How much angle is best? The research at this point suggests anything over 15 degrees may be too much, so I go for about 5 to 10 degrees. The main point here is that hanger high is generally weaker; the biggest strength gain comes from having the screw at 90 degrees to the load, with smaller strength gains coming with the hanger lower. That said, in "bad" ice (see below) it may make more sense to rely on the picket effect (same as a snow picket) and use a negative, or hanger high, angle. The strength of picket-style screws is questionable.

If you don't have the correct length screw and must use a longer-than-appropriate screw, tie it off only if it sticks out more than 5 centimeters (see Figure 7a). Tied-off screws generally fail as the ice fractures around the head and the tube bends; the tie-off sling then slides down to the hanger, which often cuts the sling before the screw fails. If the head is sticking out less than 5 centimeters, clip the stronger hanger (see Figure 7b). With more than 5 centimeters of screw sticking out the leverage becomes very high; it may be better to tie it off. Research suggests it's always better to use the correct length screw, so carry some shorter screws. Note that if the screw is a 10cm "stubbie" screw

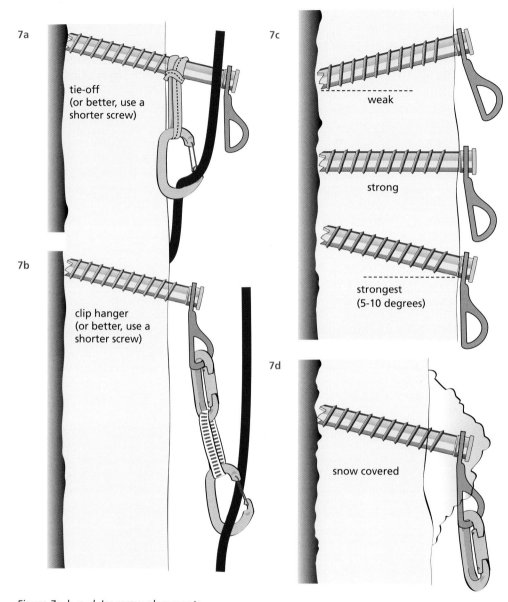

Figure 7a, b, c, d. Ice screw placements

then it will have a lot of leverage on it if you don't tie it off; I tend to tie these very short screws off if they are sticking out more than about 2 centimeters. There are no absolute rules in ice screw protection; try to understand the physics and do your best.

Place your screws in ice that is as dense, cold, and bonded to the rock as possible (see the "Ice Formation: Understanding the Medium" section in Chapter 3, Basic Ice Climbing). Dense ice is generally clearer or bluer than aerated or sunbaked ice. (Some ice with a lot of minerals or leached organics can be brown but still dense.) White ice is generally not very dense. I try to figure out how the ice formed before placing a screw. This is a fun mental game to play at belays while the leader sweats it out and you contemplate becoming one with the ice. For example, onion-skin ice layers often form on ledges after snowstorms (the ice reflows over the snow). Ice that forms slowly (steady, small quantities of water) at a consistent temperature will usually be higher quality than a stream frozen midfall during a sudden cold snap. Horizontal or lower-angle ice usually forms in sheets like a hockey rink and is generally denser and better formed than vertical or overhanging ice, which usually starts as icicles and then fills in.

Look for good ice behind pillars or other features; not only will the ice be denser but it will also be shaded from the sun. Ice that goes through strong freeze/thaw cycles seldom maintains much integrity. Sunbaked ice will often have good ice anywhere from an inch to a foot under the top layer—dig

Place screws behind pillars for thicker, more solid ice.

until you find it. A screw placed in the top layer of sunbaked ice is often worthless.

Judge the quality of the ice as you turn the screw; there should be even resistance, and the ice core coming out the tube should be homogenous. If the screw starts spinning very easily as it hits an air or junk ice pocket—find a better place. If the hanger hits protruding ice before the tube is fully buried, break the offending ice away until you can sink the screw to the hilt. If the sun is shining, do your best to find shaded ice or cover the screw with snow (see Figure 7d); direct sun on a screw can melt it out surprisingly quickly. If the screw is loose in the hole, the threads aren't engaging. All of these factors also apply to V-threads.

Enhance a stance with your foot . . .

or with your ice tool

I look at ice climbs with the idea that there are protection zones followed by climbing zones. Before leading up a climb I try to build a mental picture of where I'm likely to get good screws (protection zones), what the easiest or most interesting path will be to climb (climbing zones), and where I'm going to belay. If you start thinking about placing a screw only when the last one is vanishing into the distance below your feet, you're not planning enough. The zone idea helps me focus my efforts. The quality of the available ice should be the first thing you're thinking about, followed by how far it is to the next likely good-protection zone.

Very few ice climbs, even the really hard ones, are totally smooth sheets of vertical ice. Usually there are bumps and other features to stand on. These can be enhanced either by deepening the protrusion by kicking just above it with a sideways wiping movement of your crampon or sometimes by reaching down and enlarging it with your ice tool. (See above photos) I seldom place ice screws while standing directly on my frontpoints in the middle of a vertical shield—this is really tiring! Just getting one crampon sideways to the ice takes most of the load off your calves and arms. On even high-angle climbs a few quick whacks with the ice tool, while seeming as archaic as chopping steps, can create a nice little step to stand on.

Okay, so you've got a good stance with good ice; now it's time to fire in a screw.

I like to follow roughly the same system each time I place a screw.

1. Place one tool very solidly; this is your belay while putting in the screw. Clean off any poor surface ice, then make a small quarter-sized divot; two quick hits with the ice pick in an X pattern work well. (See Photo 4-1) This divot really helps start the ice screw cleanly. I always lead ice either with leashes that I can easily get in and out of, even if the tools are over my head, or with leashless tools; nothing makes placing screws easier.

2. Place the other tool solidly at the same horizontal level but about two feet away from the first tool at slightly less than arm's reach. (See Photo 4-2) Don't place them too close together as one may shatter the other out. I've practiced placing screws enough that I'm very comfortable placing screws with either hand; this isn't that hard, but a lot of ice climbers never learn this skill; it's worth having. If you don't have clip leashes, place the second tool as high as you can and still get out of the leash.

3. All screws should be placed at about belly-button level, and either directly in front of the climber or just barely off to the side of the waist. Many

Photo 4-1

Photo 4-2

novice climbers mistakenly try to place screws higher or farther to the side than this, but screws start only with a good continuous push while first biting into the ice. Unfortunately, this push of the screw into the ice also tends to push the climber off the wall and place outward force on the pick, which can be a problem. Place the screw close to your waist in your divot and the whole game gets a lot easier and more secure. (See Photo 4-3) Never pound a modern screw with your ice tool to get it started; this will damage the teeth and threads.

4. Hold the screw with the head in your palm and the hanger between thumb and forefinger, cock your wrist to get more rotation, and then push solidly on it with your palm while turning it. In hard ice (or with dull screws) it may take a couple of pushes to get the screw's threads "seated" during the first quarter revolution; relax and get the job done right. Now the screw is sticking out of the ice, but it's still delicate. Reset your palm for the hanger's new position and keep turning until at least one or two full threads are well engaged with the ice.

5. Only then is it safe to switch to the coffee-grinder position and send it all the way in. (See Photo 4-4) Be slow and methodical while placing screws; attempting to slam it in quickly and get moving again almost always takes more time.

If you start to pump out while placing a screw, reach back up to your free tool, clip or put your hand back into the leash, release the other hand, shake out the pumped hand, and then try again. If you climb with leashes that are difficult to get in and out of you will need to place one tool low enough to get out of the leash with either your teeth or whatever system the tool uses; this is a real hassle, and if you get pumped on your "hanging" hand, you'll have to get back into the leash and place the free tool before you can rest the pumped hand. On low-angle

Photo 4-3

Photo 4-4

tested and designed; I don't feel confident with other brands. (I'm not sponsored by Yates.) There is debate about how much force a Screamer™ can absorb, but I've tested and researched them and feel they reduce the impact enough to be worthwhile.

Never put ice screws into free-hanging ice of any size. Free-hanging ice breaks unpredictably and relatively often, and you do not want to be leashed by your ice screws to a large chunk of ice. The same rule goes for freestanding pillars unless they are the size of a bus. Even then they can still fall down, but if that happens you'll have bigger issues to worry about! I often see nervous-looking leaders placing screws in thin pillars; this is dangerous.

As soon as you remove ice screws, clean the ice out of them by banging them on the ice with the head low. Most screws have a very slight internal taper from tip to hanger, which helps clear the screw. Don't jam your pick into the tube to help clear the ice; this just makes scratches on the inner wall that the ice will stick to in the future (think Teflon™ frying pans). If you clean a screw immediately after taking it out, the ice will seldom stick. If it does and you can't get it out, try holding the screw vertically with the tip up and banging the hanger end on the head of your hammer; this will often loosen the plug in small steps until it all falls out. If that doesn't work, try starting a screw hole with another screw, then screwing the clogged screw into the hole until the ice plug moves; often just getting it to move a little bit solves the problem. If that doesn't work, you'll have to warm the

routes this is fine, but get some good clip leashes or leashless tools for the steep rigs.

Sometimes it's a good idea to clip the rope in to your high tool with a quickdraw while placing a screw; a lot of people seem to fall off when placing screws, probably because they don't really set their tool and because they try to place a screw too high. Clip in to the hole in the spike, not the hole in the head.

I always put a Yates Screamer™ on the first screw off the belay, where the impact forces will be highest, and on most screws in general. Yates Screamers™ are carefully screw up enough to break the ice/metal bond. I'll put really frozen screws into the chest pocket of my jacket. Usually I forget about them and get wet, but at least then the screw is working again.

If the ice is at all questionable I'll often place two or even three screws and equalize all of them. Running it out for 15 meters on a set of screws you have good faith in is often a better strategy than placing one questionable screw every 5 or 10 meters. You may find fixed V-threads left by other parties retreating down your line; I always clip these, but often back them up by placing a quick screw nearby and equalizing both. For greater security, clip the rope into the V-thread while you place the screw.

The jury is still out on whether or not old holes are okay to use for new screws. In general, if there's enough ice, place a new one. The climber before you may have used a larger-diameter screw, in which case the threads won't hold.

On many climbs you can get a very solid piece of protection by simply walking around a pillar or other large feature and continuing on up. The ice behind pillars is often very good, so I'll often place a screw on a long runner behind the pillar and walk around it. This protection scenario never fails to make me feel secure.

Ice hooks are common, and there are times when they are reportedly quite strong. However, with the advent of short screws and a better understanding of screw physics, most climbers are using hooks less and less. Never use ice hooks of any variety as the first piece on a route—they zipper out very easily. (Use an ice screw as the first piece; it's an omnidirectional anchor.) How strong is an ice hook? That's the big question. The research so far indicates that it's very hard to tell how strong an ice hook is, much harder than with a screw. A hook requires at least 4 inches of solid ice to be effective, so why not just use an ice screw or, if it's a thin curtain, an I-thread (see the "Thin Ice Protection" section in Chapter 6, Advanced Ice Technique)? I use ice hooks mainly as mixed protection; they work great in mossy, dirty, or iced-up cracks where nothing else will. Some people use ice hooks in free-hanging ice on the theory that if the ice breaks then the hooks will fall out instead of lashing the climber to the now free-falling ice. This may be a good use for them if the leader takes a mild slip and if the rope doesn't flip the hook out and if the hook is solid enough to hold the fall. That's a lot of ifs.

MULTIPITCH ANCHORS

In general I use two but sometimes up to five screws on a multipitch belay—the number is less important than being absolutely sure that the belay will hold me, my partner, and my import pickup truck. The truck weighs about 3000 pounds and it's possible to generate that much force in a hard fall onto the belay, so I visualize hanging my truck off the belay and ask myself, "Would I be okay with that?" Two 19cm equalized screws buried to the hilt in bomber ice give me a good feeling of security, but if one of them feels "off" for

Use a cordelette to efficiently equalize anchor points.

belay screws at 90 degrees to the expected load; remember that the force on a belay screw may be "up" rather than down, so a compromise is in order. However, the most violent fall possible would be a factor-two right onto the belay, so I leave it equalized for this event rather than for an upward pull.

A cordelette is the preferred system for equalizing a multipiece belay; slings will work in a pinch, but equalized anchors work well only if they are truly equalized—this is

Three bomber screws equalized with a cordelette = security.

whatever reason I'll add more anchors until I feel totally secure. Don't be hesitant to find another belay if you can't get good gear. At some point the belay will be your sole anchor to life, so make it truly bomb-proof and don't accept "That's good enough; he's not going to fall anyhow." This is how people get killed.

Place the belay screws at least 1 or 2 feet apart and offset vertically, rather than side by side. Belay screws should always be at least 12 inches apart—more if the ice is at all suspect; ice tends to fracture horizontally under load. I usually place

Figure 8. The "American triangle" is not recommended for linking anchors as it increases the load on both anchors. it also shocks loads the remaining anchor should one anchor fail.

hard to do well with slings. Do not use the popular but dangerous "American Triangle" (see Figure 8). Loop the cordelette through all the carabiners and then tie it with a figure-eight knot that equalizes the forces on the anchor. The idea is that even if one piece blows, the others won't be shock loaded. This knot is commonly called the "power point" or "focal point" as all systems move off this. I like 8mm cord; it has a high breaking strength (up to 14 kilonewtons [kN], more force than a rope will generate during a hard fall) yet it's dynamic and so will help reduce the impact on the belay anchors. Cord also stretches a lot before it breaks; this will help equalize the falling force if the pull doesn't come from the direction you anticipated, as well as absorb some of the impact force. Webbing doesn't do this.

Using the ever-popular "twisted sling" means that if one piece blows, the other will be shock loaded.

LEADING THE PITCH

On the first belayed pitch the belayer should stand to the side of potential ice falling from the leader or find a fully protected nook under the leader. There are a couple of schools of thought on whether or not the belayer should be anchored to the ground. The first school feels that all belayers should be anchored at all times; this keeps the belayer from being pulled across the ground and into the air and also shortens the total length of the leader's fall. (If the belayer moves four feet, the leader falls an additional eight.) The second school feels that anchoring the belayer increases the impact force on the lead screw; the motion of the belayer spreads the impact force out over more time, reducing the peak impact force on the lead screw. In general, I anchor the belayer well off to the side for the first pitch if I'm worried about a pillar or free-hanging icicle falling onto the belayer. It's impossible for a belayer to hold a fall and stay stationary well off to the side if unanchored; if he gets sucked into the impact zone then that's bad for the belayer and possibly the leader.

Impact forces are generally more relevant in ice climbing than on rock; minimizing the forces on questionable ice pro is a good idea. Very thin half ropes have a relatively low-impact force (4.9kN) compared to a fat single rope (7.2kN for a 10.5mm rope tested for a single-rope lead fall). However, thin ropes obviously stretch more. See the "Ropes" section in Chapter 1, Gear, for more ideas on this topic and make your own decision—it's personal and opinions are strong. Check the websites for more ideas. I like two half ropes for long alpine routes and single ropes with a separate rap line for long ice routes, but this is one of those decisions in climbing that has good arguments for both systems.

When belaying a leader, always clip in to the focal point with your rope and belay off your harness, not directly off the anchor. If you have two feet of rope leading into the anchor and a cordelette, you dramatically reduce the impact if the leader takes a factor-two fall straight onto the belay. To illustrate this, imagine what happens if the leader climbs six feet above your belay device and then whips; the resulting fall will be roughly twelve feet with only six feet in the system. However, if you have a 2-foot piece of rope in the system between you and the anchor, there is actually 8 feet of rope in the system, which greatly reduces the impact force. More impact force is taken up by the belayer's body, the minimal but very helpful movement of the rope through the belay device during the fall, and the stretch of the cordelette. In contrast, if you clip a Grigri™ directly in to webbing attached to the anchors, there is exactly 6 feet of rope available for the 12-foot fall and no shock-absorbing "give" anywhere in the anchor system. A factor-two fall in this situation will be very violent and hard on the belay anchors.

Popular wisdom suggests that it's a good idea to clip the leader's rope in to the top screw in the belay anchor as he heads out from the belay. I have mixed feelings about this system for a couple of reasons. First, when the leader falls the belayer will likely be sucked up tight against the upper screw, putting all the load on it as the lead climber falls past and slams onto the end of the rope. Now you have close to a factor-two fall straight onto one screw. Second, as the belay device hits the carabiner on the top screw it may be difficult for the belayer to keep all his fingers intact and retain control of the rope. On the other hand, the belayer's movement up to the top screw will spread the impact over time, which reduces the force. If the climbing straight off the belay is sketchy and the high screw in the anchor system inspires total confidence, I'll clip the leader's rope in to it for the first 5 or 6 feet of climbing, then unclip it after this point when the loads start to become violent in the event of a fall. In general, it's safest for the leader to put in a good solid screw no more than a couple of meters out from the belay, especially if he is going to run it out a long way between screws low on the pitch.

If you've really screwed up and have questions about the solidity of the anchor but there is absolutely nothing to be done about it (note: this is a really bad situation), clip a Screamer™ between you and the focal point. (Back this up with a loop of rope clove-hitched in to the focal point as an

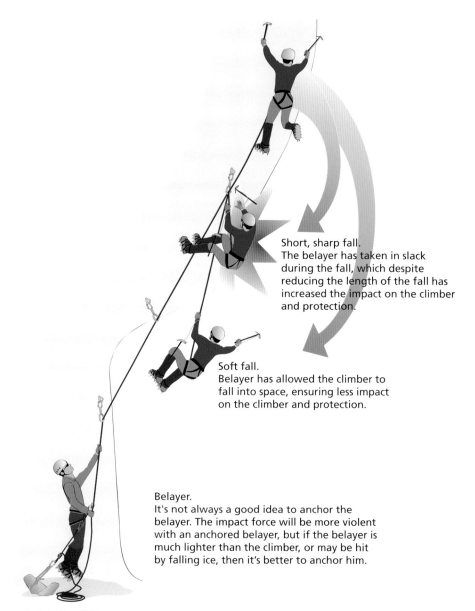

Short, sharp fall.
The belayer has taken in slack during the fall, which despite reducing the length of the fall has increased the impact on the climber and protection.

Soft fall.
Belayer has allowed the climber to fall into space, ensuring less impact on the climber and protection.

Belayer.
It's not always a good idea to anchor the belayer. The impact force will be more violent with an anchored belayer, but if the belayer is much lighter than the climber, or may be hit by falling ice, then it's better to anchor him.

Figure 9. Catching falls

A nice sheltered cave = all-time favorite belay spot

opened Screamer™ is not extremely strong.) All of this might seem overly paranoid, but a little paranoia may save both your lives if the leader suddenly goes sailing by the belay or rips all the gear above the belay. There are amazing stories of two people falling onto one screw while simulclimbing and having it hold, but trusting in blind luck is seldom a good idea in the mountains.

If the belay anchor is bomber (and it should be), it's often easier and more pleasant to belay the second up on a Petzl Reverso™ or a plaquette clipped directly in to the focal point; this allows the leader to eat, drink, put on more clothes, or what-

ever while the second is secure. It's also easy to belay two seconds with either of these devices.

Many novice ice climbers stretch their rope to the end and then slap in a belay. It's possible to build a secure ice belay almost anywhere on a fat ice line, but this strategy ignores the belayer who may be seriously unhappy if continuously smacked with falling ice on the next pitch! I've often winced with empathy watching a novice team build belay after belay where the belayer is directly below the climber. Try to set belays in logical places: if you're climbing an 80-meter route and there's a good belay at 30 meters, stop and do the next pitch as a 50-meter unit rather running it out the full length of the rope and missing a solid, protected belay.

I like to belay in caves, behind curtains, or in nooks that offer good ice and good protection for the belayer. Sometimes a curtain will hide a nice cave with a flat, comfy floor. A few high-aggression minutes with an ice tool can often punch a hole through the curtain and into the hidden room; this is my all-time favorite belay spot as it totally protects the belayer from falling ice, wind, and water and almost always has good ice—plus it's a lot warmer to belay where you can stand on flat ground rather than while semihanging.

Changeovers between the leader and second should be safe and fast and involve a minimum of the ever-possible Flustersnarl factor. As you belay the second up, stack the rope neatly; caves often have nice flat floors allowing the leader to stack the rope cleanly—but if not then stack it over the rope from your harness to the anchor, on your foot, or in your pack. Double ropes should be stacked separately if at all possible; they seem to snarl much easier than singles, especially with a good coat of ice on them. As the second approaches, move to the side; and if you have one, clip a locking carabiner in to the focal point, then clip the second's rope in to the 'biner. The more a climbing team can share the work harmoniously and with good humor the more efficiently they will move. If you can cut your changeovers to five minutes each from fifteen, it's possible to save over an hour on a six-pitch route; being down at the base of the route as it gets dark is always more pleasant than finishing the last pitch just as it gets dark.

As the leader heads out from the belay he or she should place a good screw in the first 10 feet or so if possible. The leader should already have had a good look up and figured out a rough plan, which should then be communicated to the belayer if the belayer can't see up the route, with something like "The ice looks lousy, but I think I can get some screws off to the side and belay after about 150 feet or so on the big ledge we saw from the ground. OK, give her." The leader then heads out, sending down the usual debris. When there's about 30 feet of rope the second should yell "30 feet!" If the leader can hear the second, he should yell "OK!" This warning should be repeated at "10 feet!" Keep communication short and simple; yelling down "I think I can reach a belay in about 30 feet and get off!" can easily be misconstrued as "I'm at the belay and off!"

Once the leader establishes a solid belay he should yell down "Off!" This means he is no longer relying on the belayer and is on his own program. The belayer should yell back "OK, belay off!" only if absolutely sure the leader said "Off!" If the belayer is not sure, he should keep the leader on belay until there is no more rope. Once the leader has the belay organized he starts pulling up the loose rope; when it goes tight on the second, the second yells "That's me!" The leader then puts the second on and yells "On belay!" The second then strips the belay and yells "Climbing!" The leader yells back "Climb!" In Canada and some other countries climbers use the word "Secure" for "Off." It doesn't matter which word is used, just that it's clear and understood between both climbers. If you are climbing with a new partner—especially a new partner who doesn't speak your language—then a minute spent figuring out signals can save a real communication clusterfuck.

If it's windy there may be no verbal communication at all between the leader and second; good teams will easily deal with this as normal, while weaker teams will epic. The typical program goes like this: The belayer can usually tell when the leader is getting a belay in as the rope will be stationary for a long period of time, then move out quite quickly as the leader pulls the extra rope up after establishing a belay. If the leader is still climbing, the rope will move in short jerks. If the rope stops moving for a long time, then moves up quickly (the second still has it on belay just in case), then stops as the rope goes tight on the belayer (the belayer still yells "That's me!"), then goes tight again on the second, the leader has probably put the second on belay and is waiting for him to climb. Repeated short pulls from the leader on the rope will confirm this. The second breaks the belay down and heads up. However, if the rope has slowly but continuously been moving out and the leader hits the end of the rope and pulls it tight, both climbers have some decisions to make. The belayer should yell "That's all!" and wait to see if the leader keeps pulling for more rope or downclimbs to a possible belay (the rope will go slack; take it in).

If the leader keeps pulling on the rope with no communication, the second then has two options: sit tight and make the leader put in a belay either where he is or lower, or break down the belay and start climbing. This is where trust in your partner comes in. If you trust the leader to make good decisions, start climbing with the assumption that the terrain is relatively easy for you and him, and that he just needs a few more feet to reach a perfect belay. However, if you think the leader is prone to bad decision making, you shouldn't be out with him in the first place. The integrity of a partnership is only as good as the trust and understanding between the two climbers. I'll trust almost anybody to hold my rope in the climbing gym for a few burns, but for ice climbing I want a real partner that I fully trust.

BARRY BLANCHARD WHIPS ICE CLIMBING

After 25 years of ice climbing it finally happened. Today I fell onto an ice screw. It happened in Johnston Canyon. Catherine and I had walked in with Finnigan—the Irish sled dog—and my beautiful wife had warmed us up leading a WI 4 pitch. My lead, I walked the half-height catwalk to its north end eyeing a stout pillar up the far corner, then out a meter-and-a-half roof to finish in the trees. I chimneyed up between rock and the solid pillar, placing six screws (three in series at the top to safeguard the hard pull through the roof). Must have been too hard because I went at it once and decided that the better way to solve the problem was to step across space to a "just" touched-down pillar to the south. I placed another good screw before stepping out. I turned onto that pillar's front, tight under a one-meter roof that had formed, like the other I'd abandoned, by the perfect horizontal shearing of large bygone pillars. I bridged my right foot wide to tag a 30-foot goatee that had formed over the old one-meter truncation. At least one other person had climbed here. A couple of hard cranks with the left tool in the old ice top of the bygone pillar and delicate tapping with my right tool in the goatee and I got my left foot over the roof and I thought that it was over and that it hadn't actually been that hard, many good rests.

I was getting stable in order to place another screw. *Tap, tap, tap* with my right tool, *thunck,* and then a lightning strike opening the ice and running upslope by my right tool! A hideous tearing sound like metal ripping and me thinking, "OK, here we go!" A flash of 30 feet and a number of thousands of pounds of ice plunging away; a violent tug, then me sailing sideways and down.

Absolute thunder, my back arching as the rope caught me . . . softly.

"Barry! Barry! Are you OK, Barry?"

"Ya, I'm OK."

"You're coming down right now! I don't want to climb in this fucking place! We're getting out of here!" Catherine lowered me and I thought that I had both tools, but when my feet hit the ground I saw that my left tool was gone and that the wristband was still closed tight around my wrist and that all eight bar-tacks that attach it via two strands of ½-inch black webbing had blown!

I went back up with one of Catherine's tools and cleaned the pitch, lowering off of one screw and a locking 'biner. Catherine found my left tool in the jumble of debris at the base. A small silver-metal ladder lock used to hold the excess strapping against the micro 'biner of the "Liberty" leash was gone and 4 inches of doubled webbing had run through the one-centimeter slot at the base of the micro and stoppered. My back, shoulders, and abdominals took a torquing. The fracture ran up from me for six feet, then across the very top of the goatee for an arching 10 feet. The crown was one and one-half feet deep and the fracture stepped down into the old stub to a depth of one and one-half meters. I think my right tool snagged in the parting ice, which pitched me into a horizontal crucifix and the weight shot through my wingspan and exploded the small ladder lock, the doubled webbing ran through the micro under pressure and hit its end, then the bar tacks ripped in series on both sides of my wrist and I was airborne. I think the recoil on my left tool popped it free to fall.

Catherine was lifted about four feet until she snapped tight to her ground anchor, slam-dancing her knee into the pillar—great things, those ground anchors, when ice is filling the sky. She allowed no rope to slip through her ATC.

I was caught largely by one of the half ropes (obvious from the far superior tension in that knot at my harness), I'd alternated clipping on the way up. I was caught on Grivel's shortest "360 Ultimate" ice screw (12cm) and a half-inch Wild Things sewn spectra single runner and two Lucky™ carabiners. The screw was in good ice on top of the first pillar and it hadn't moved at all, with no powdering of the ice below the screw. I estimate the fall factor at about .5 as I came to rest in space about 10 feet above Catherine. I think that I took about a 25-foot fall on 55 feet of rope, but it may have been 30 feet on 65 or 70 feet of rope. The half rope, used properly, did a grand job.

On sober reflection, I figure the climbing was hard WI 5 and that 8000 pounds (seriously) cut loose. I was hoping to get through having never fallen onto a screw, c'est la dic.

I can now state from experience that it all works!

— *Barry Blanchard*

CHAPTER 5

Descending after the first ascent of Howse Peak, Banff National Park, Canada (Photo © Scott Semple)

Descending

My partners and I celebrate a climb only when we're back at the car. Although the ascent is arduous, the descent is often more serious. On the ascent we're keyed up, focused, and fresh; on the descent we're tired, slower, and more prone to make a series of errors that could lead to an accident. A safe descent starts well before the ascent by leaving enough time to descend in the light; having enough food to stay strong and enough warm clothes to be comfortable; and having solid, well-practiced systems in place before the top of the climb. Most ice climbs are done during the short days of winter, so plan to either finish well before dark or be comfortable moving in the dark. I hate getting out of bed early, but it's generally better to be back in town at two o'clock in the afternoon laughing about how fast you were than to be shivering on a ledge at two o'clock in the morning because you couldn't find the rap anchor in the dark.

Routefinding on most ice climbs is pretty obvious; you go up the ice or connect the ice bits if it's a mixed climb. Descents are more complicated: usually you go back down the ice, but often there is a walk-off, rap anchors are already set in the rock beside the climb, or perhaps nobody can descend the route midday due to avalanche risk. After several notable epics I now read the descent section of the guidebook with a greedy eye for specific information: how many raps, where the stations are, alternatives, and so on. I like to ask somebody who has actually done the route about the descent; often the guidebook information is outdated, nonexistent, or wrong. As you climb the route, build a descent plan; mentally record good sheltered places to place threads, note existing anchors, remember hazards such as large hanging ice daggers, and link these features together so you arrive at the top of the route with a clear idea of what you're going to do next.

Descending off single-pitch climbs is usually straightforward. If it's a well-traveled climb, there's probably a fixed anchor. Evaluate the rap anchor carefully, paying special attention to the cord and anchor points. If it's not bomber, create a new one; every year a handful of climbers around the world die from blown rap anchors. This sort of accident is one of the more avoidable in climbing. If in doubt, leave gear. Climbers, even sponsored climbers, are often cheap but leaving an extra nut, sling, or even in a worst-case scenario an ice screw is inexpensive insurance.

If you're an active climber then it's likely that over the years you'll find about as much gear as you leave or more than you leave anyhow. I've had several friends die or deal with severe injuries after rap anchors blew; I'm definitely over finding satisfaction in rapping off bad gear to save a few dollars.

Rap anchors are composed of a primary anchor (whatever you plan to leave) and if at all possible a solid backup anchor. The primary anchor should be equalized like a normal belay. (Don't use an American Triangle! See Figure 8 in Chapter 4, Anchors, Belaying, and Leading) I'll rap off a two-bolt station with fresh sling without a backup anchor, but I back up all threads, pins, and so on. For example, if you create a V-thread (see "Abalakovs," below), place a bomber ice screw to the side and clip this screw in to the ropes with a sling and two carabiners for the first person. Make sure the screw isn't taking any weight, just backing the whole situation up (see Figure 10). Send the heaviest person first while the anchor is backed up. The last person pulls the backup piece. Again,

Ice screw back-up shouldn't be taking any weight.

Figure 10: An Abalakov being used as a rap anchor. The ice screw back-up is removed before the final climber rappels.

each other (tube-style belay devices do this automatically; figure 8s don't). When you unclip your device, be careful to keep the strands from twisting; most rap problems start with just one little twist on the strands.

I like to be clipped in at all rap stations, even if I'm standing on a big ledge. This may seem paranoid, but even a small slough coming down a gully could easily blow a climber off a big ledge. After all the climbers are down and ready to pull the rope, make sure that everyone is in a safe position in case the rope knocks down more ice or rock. On multipitch routes or routes with a confined area below the rap, the first climber down should clear out any icicles, curtains, loose rock, or anything that could fall as the others rap. There's nothing worse than gingerly rapping past a big icicle and then realizing that you've got to wait under it as the next two climbers come down. Remove icicles or anything else that could fall on the climbers below (assuming that doing so doesn't jeopardize climbers below you).

Teamwork is critical for descents; everyone should work well together to keep the process moving. I usually do a long rappel descent with one person doing all the anchor building and the others assisting. On multipitch routes the first climber to rap sets the next anchor and stays on the rap ropes until the anchor is fully built, then he bounce-tests the anchor (clips in to the focal point with a sling and "bounces" on it) hard before calling "Off!" The anchor builder should also loosely clip the rap ropes in to that new anchor to keep control of them and for added safety.

make the primary anchor bomber.

After the first climber raps, she should give the rope a test pull, even if it appears the rope will "obviously run fine." Those are famous last words before an epic starts—test the pull. Verbalize which rope to pull if using double ropes: "Pulling blue!" If you pull the wrong rope, it's easy for the knot to get hung up in the anchor even if the climber suddenly remembers which rope was the correct one to pull. As you rap, keep the strands from twisting over

A good rap anchor should be absolutely bomber, totally out of the way of debris coming down from above, and positioned so that the ropes will pull well on the next rap. Finding anchors that meet all these criteria is important; meeting all three often means making a shorter rap, but two short raps that pull well are far faster than one long one that ends in the middle of the gully with bad ice and where the rope won't pull well.

If the ropes are frozen or icy, it may be a good idea to use a prusik or other backup, especially with very thin ropes. I use one knot for both ends of the rope when

WHAT TO DO IF THE ROPES GET STUCK

If you're on the ground, walk back away from the climb as far as possible or to the side and try to pull the rope again; often just changing the angle of pull will be enough to solve the problem. It may be useful to clip in to it with a knot so you can really pull on it; sometimes having two or three people pulling will break the rope free if it's frozen into place. (This can be humorous on flat ground but dangerous on steep terrain.) If you're hanging at an anchor midway down a climb and the rope won't pull, try flipping the ropes aggressively. Something has obviously changed because you test-pulled the rope (right?) before the last person came down. If you pulled the rope and it got stuck midway or hung up on the way down, you're either abandoning what's still above you or climbing back up to unstick it if possible.

If the rope started to pull and then stuck with one end near the anchor, you should have a lot of free rope. Tie in to the hanging rope (bowline on a bight or other mid-rope knot) and have your partner put you on belay, put a prusik on the stuck rope for a sliding self-belay, and lead back up, placing screws or other protection as you normally would on lead. Be sure to clip this protection in to the rope that runs to your harness, not in to the loop of rope that's hanging from the anchor. The prusik on the stuck rope provides some mental security but should not be trusted to hold a fall. Don't batman the stuck rope in a surge of rage; it may become unstuck suddenly as the angle of pull changes as you near the stuck point.

If the rope just refuses to pull while both strands are at the belay, tie one side off to the rap anchor (or have your partner tie it off to her harness if you're on the ground), put a prusik or Petzl Tiblock™ on the other side, and climb back up, periodically backing yourself up with a knot so that if your prusik blows you don't fall all the way back down the climb. If the rope is free-hanging and running through a sling (not a carabiner) at the top, consider using a prusik on both strands of the rope; that way the rope won't run over the sling with your weight on it due to rope stretch, if you fall. A loaded rope running on a sling can cut it in just a few feet. Figure out what the problem was, fix it, have your partner test- pull again, rap, and ideally things will work better the second go.

rapping into unfamiliar territory, especially at night when it's hard to see the ends of the rope. Individual knots on each rope cause less twisting, but I've had problems at night with forgetting to take out the second knot when I'm tired. Keep control of both strands of the rope as you complete the pull, carefully checking that the strand of rope moving up to the high anchor is knot-free. I've had the rope tie itself into over-hand knots many times. Feed the end of the rope you're pulling through the current anchor as you pull it; this saves time and reduces rope clusterfucks.

I like to rap with a sling girth-hitched in to my belay loop and clip it in to the rap anchor with a locking carabiner. Daisy chains are common too, but be very sure that you're not clipped through one tack. Because ice climbing often involves dark, cold, and weird situations, I don't use daisy chains. They are just one more thing that can go wrong.

RAP ANCHORS

Building good rap anchors is a critical skill for those climbing multipitch routes. Never assume that an existing anchor is bomber; it may have been created in very different conditions from what you find (a large block well attached to the wall with ice one day may be too melted out to be solid the next). Paranoia is a good thing on descents. Bring lots of cord for building complicated anchors; on a descent down the 4000-foot face of Howse Peak, my partners and I used at least 40 feet of cord. An old carabiner or

rap ring will greatly reduce the amount of force required to pull the ropes. After dark or in other situations where retrieving a stuck cord would be serious, I tend to leave old carabiners or a rap ring on rap anchors. No matter what type of anchor is used, back it up for the first person to rap and have the heaviest person rap first. Bounce-test all rap anchors while still on belay to the last rap anchor. Remember that the forces on rap anchors can be tremendous if you're hit with a slide or part of it blows with three people hanging on it—build good ones!

ABALAKOVS

The Abalakov, named for its Russian inventor, Valerie Abalakov, is often essential for descending ice climbs or alpine routes. An Abalakov, also know as a V-thread or Billy Bob, is very strong in good ice, often stronger than the cord used. As rappel anchors they are unbeatable; it's easy to carry enough thread material to rap many pitches, and with practice they are fast and safe.

The basic idea is to create two angled ice-screw holes that connect at least 6 inches under the surface of the ice. I always carry one 22cm screw to create the holes. Although research suggests that even very shallow V-threads can be strong, I like the security of a thick, good piece of ice connecting the holes. A little bit of a paranoid attitude toward rap anchors is probably a good thing; more climbers die on rap than at any other time.

To prepare for placing V-threads, take a couple of long screws and hold them up in a V with the tips touching; see what the angles look like and how changing the angles affects the amount of ice that would be between the heads of the screws. I've found it really helps to understand how the system works and what angles create the "nicest," or equilateral, piece of triangular ice. Practice making V-threads somewhere comfortable, like on a frozen lake. It's a lot better to figure it all out standing around on flat ground with a cup of coffee than in the dark at the end of the ropes on a vertical pitch of ice.

Abalakovs are best placed in ice that you think would hold a good screw. Any good piece of well-attached ice will work, but I get the best results with ice on the lips of drops or other places where it has flowed very uniformly.

Start the first hole with the screw at about 45 degrees to the surface of the ice and bury it to the hilt. (See Photo 5-1) If it hits air pockets or water, find a new place for the thread. Water-laden ice can be very weak, and air pockets are obviously bad too. Remove the screw, have a look in the hole, and then place

another screw into the already made hole for just a few threads. This helps you visualize where the hole went into the ice as you make the second hole.

Start the second hole with the screw at 90 degrees to the ice and at the proper horizontal distance from the first hole to create an equilateral triangle. (See Photo 5-2) If you have a hard time guessing the correct distance, take another 21 cm screw and hold it flat on the ice; starting the holes a bit closer together than the length of the screw guarantees an equilateral triangle. The reason to start it at 90 degrees instead of 45 degrees is that a screw at 45 degrees will "skate" across the ice toward the first hole, reducing the distance between the holes; this is a common error. If you start the first hole at 90 degrees and create a small "pocket" about one thread deep, you'll have the right distance. After the screw creates a small pocket, turn it 45 degrees, eyeball the other screw sticking out of the hole carefully to visualize your trajectory,

Photo 5-1

Photo 5-2

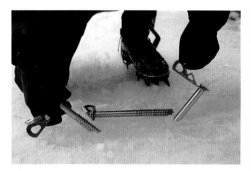

Photo 5-3

and then screw it in. (See Photo 5-3) If all's gone well the screw will be buried at least two-thirds of the way before it intersects the other hole. After the second screw is turning well, take the first one out of its hole and look down it to see the second screw intersect the hole. If it intersects only midway down the hole, start over with a new V-thread. If the distance between the two holes isn't close to the length of the screws used, start over.

Assuming that the second hole intersected well toward the bottom of the first hole, then you're good to insert the cord or webbing. I like to use a minimum of 7mm cord; a loop of good 7mm cord should test at over 3000 pounds, more than enough for a rap anchor. Pieces of old 8.1mm ropes make bomber thread anchors, although they do require slightly more accurate holes. I find cord generally goes into the hole better than tubular webbing does, plus cord is far more resistant to abrasion than webbing. If you're rapping on two different-size ropes, it's possible that the rope may pull over the thread material for a long distance; nylon on nylon creates a lot of

heat, and nylon melts at a very low temperature. Often other parties may use your threads, so it's courtesy to use good cord. Before inserting the cord, place your mouth over the first hole and blow hard; this shoots all the loose bits of ice out and makes threading the Abalakov much easier. Insert the cord into the hole that is higher at the intersection and hook it back out the other hole with your "hooker." (See Photo 5-4) If you've blown it and can't hook the cord even though you can see it, you have two options: start the whole process again or modify one hole using the same hole but starting the screw at a slightly different angle. I usually just redo one hole slightly; this shouldn't affect the strength of the ice.

Thread hookers come in a variety of shapes and sizes. The most basic is a piece of coat hanger with a sharpened, small bent hook at one end. Commercial versions are available but the idea is the same. Tie the cord with a double-fishermans knot with plenty of tail; thinner cord tends to pull through the knot for an inch or two until it is really tight. After finishing the thread,

Photo 5-4

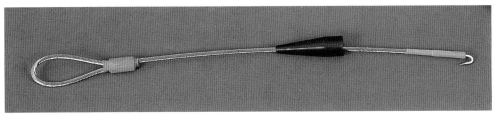

Thread hooker

clip in to it directly with a quickdraw or sling and while still on belay, bounce it hard. This sets the knot and puts a much higher load on the thread than you're likely to produce while rappeling. Make sure the thread is bomber; it'll be the only thing between you and the deck at some point.

As with all rap anchors, back up the V-thread with a good screw for the first person (send the heaviest person first). Make sure the backup screw doesn't take any of the load, because the idea is to test the integrity of the thread under a real-world scenario. Don't clip the backup in to the cord but through the ropes; if the cord fails, the backup is worthless if clipped in to the cord.

If you're rapping a route and find an in-situ V-thread, it's temping to just clip in and use it for a rap; this can be okay to do, but be sure to bounce-test the old thread thoroughly. Stay on rappel, clip in to the old thread, and really examine the cord, ice quality, and depth of holes. Abalakovs that were put in months earlier may be useless as the surface ice melts away, or they may be so frozen in that you can't figure out what part of the thread is correct to clip in to. More than one climber has died by clipping in to the frozen tail of a thread

instead of the actual thread loop. If you can't see what's going on and can't bounce-test the thread properly, create a new one.

ROCK ANCHORS

If the ice is too thin for V-threads, rock anchors are the common solution. Bolted stations are increasingly common on climbs,

especially those that see a lot of guiding traffic, but check to make sure that the bolts are in good repair. I've had several rusted bolt hangers blow out under very low loads.

Two good bolts, pins, or nuts are the minimum for me; I don't trust any one piece of gear totally. As with V-threads, back up the primary anchor and make the heaviest person go first.

TREES

Trees are often great rap anchors, but never just throw your rope over the tree and rap; pulling the rope kills the bark and eventually the tree—which you might want to use on future descents. Tying a sling around a growing tree will also kill it as the tree expands in girth over the years; climbers have killed plenty of trees in this manner due to either ignorance or laziness.

If you have to rap off a tree, loop a doubled sling around it so that it won't choke the tree after you're gone. Feed the rap rope through both "ends" of the sling so the sling is resting on the tree, rather than encircling it.

PILLARS AND TRICKY THREADS

One of the most satisfying rappels is to simply throw your rope around a large pillar and rap; these are in general bomber, but be careful rigging in. Two climbers can rap at the same time. This is efficient, but can be dangerous and tricky to set up, so it's better to just rap normally.

Some curtains can also be punched out and threaded. A 6-inch curtain is very strong, especially if it is relatively short between base and top, but as always, back it up with a good screw for the first person.

HOW TO BUILD AN ABALAKOV WITHOUT A "HOOKER."
by Joe McCay

This is a trick that I find myself doing more and more as I tend to forget to bring all the bells and whistles. There was a time I never went anywhere without my bent-up coat hanger wire, but these days I am much less likely to be carrying anything specific for placing Abalakov (Ul-bee-bac-en-off!) threads.

Materials needed: One sewn sling
One meter (or more) of 7mm perlon cord.

- Drill the Abalakov so that you get a near perfect intersection. Over-drill the second hole so that the core is at least 2 or 3 centimeters past the intersection.
- Fold the sewn sling in two.
- Push the sling loop down one hole, stopping when the tip of the loop gets just beyond the intersection. Be sure that your sling is facing the right way. It should be possible to turn it slightly once you have inserted the sewn sling.
- Take the 7mm perlon cord and push it down the second hole so that it not only intersects the sewn sling but goes beyond into the over drilled part.
- Tug slightly on the sewn sling (like you have a fish nibbling on a bait hook). Be sure to feed a little extra cord into the second core to reduce resistance.
- Pull on the sewn sling "like you're pulling a skier off your sister." The end of the cord should come flying out.

This is not near so bad as it sounds as far as finicky fishing goes.

CLUSTER LUCK

Someone with a plan will always be able to absorb the unexpected faster than the lackadaisical punter who pinballs his way through the day.

— Scott Semple

Plans are for people with too much time on their hands.

— Will Gadd

Our goal: Enchain Polar Circus (V, WI 5, 700m), the Weeping Pillar (V, WI 6, 350m), and Curtain Call (IV, WI 6, 125m) in less than 24 hours. Any one of these climbs normally takes a day to complete. On our attempt, the truck contained 12 turkey sandwiches, 14 liters of sports drinks, 6 apple turnovers, 36 energy gels, 100 cookies, and 20 cans of Red Bull™.

I spent the preclimb day nervously organizing our food, sharpening my tools and crampons, testing headlamp batteries, sorting screws, and confirming that the snow bowls above Polar Circus had been bombed. I brainstormed through each transition hoping to find a hidden speed secret or, at the very least, appease my perfectionist twinges.

I didn't talk to my partner, Will Gadd, all day. That wasn't surprising; while I deconstruct objectives, Will establishes points A and B and sees no reason why he can't draw a straight line between them. I hoped my type-A personality would mesh with Will's "It's there, climb it" approach.

Our first adventure came with a late-night drive up the Icefield Parkway. In-your-face blues or feel-good pop are my cheesy style, while Will maintains an aural stream of angst-ridden thrash metal or raving techno. We found some middle ground in Ice T.

After a couple hours of roadside sleep and a short drive from our crunchy, melt-freeze bivy site, we parked in front of Polar Circus. Bugs McKeith, Charlie Porter, and the Burgess twins completed the first ascent of Polar Circus in 1975. The skilled foursome pushed to the top in eight days. Today, most climbers are back at the car in 10 to 12 hours. It's been soloed in less than 3.

It didn't feel like 3:00 A.M. That night-before-Christmas-morning feeling and climbing with a superstar had me vibrating as much as did the Red Bull™ and turkey coursing through my veins. I smiled at my groggy companion and flicked my watch over to stopwatch mode. With a high-pitched *dee-deet,* we started moving. Fresh headlamp batteries, snow cover, and a full moon lit the way.

The sunbaked crust was barely enough to hold body weight; every fifth step was an annoying breakthrough into isothermal sugar. Nervous thoughts surfaced about the postholing pace and what that meant for the upper Weeping Wall. How are those pitches going to react to the sun? Can we get there before they're baked to unprotectable mush? We abandoned the annoying crust and traversed into the low-angled beginning of Polar Circus.

My feet tried to keep up to my ambition, and I fought my body for the first hour. Will passed me on the lower ice steps and doubt began to creep in. Am I going to be able to keep up? I kept walking as I ripped open a gel. The combined motor skills distracted my brain long enough for my body to take control and set a better pace. I fell into a mellower groove and strangely started to speed up.

Will snapped on screws and slings while I flung the rope into a quick stack. With a *click-click* of his leashes, he strode toward the first real pitch. I paid out some rope, shut off my headlamp, and smiled. The quiet black was broken by Will's confident rhythm and the pale glow from his headlamp. A jagged silhouette marked where rock and ice ended and stars began. So far, this is a good, good day.

With a tight rope above me, I abandoned the soloing technique and concentrated on speed. *Thwack.* Trust it. Don't look at your feet. Kick, kick. *Thwack.* Trust it. Don't look at your feet. Kick, kick. The familiar rhythm of swinging tools got me out of my head and into my body; moving over ice was comforting and temporarily hid my reservations.

Clip the anchor, pass the gear, nod and smile, on belay, go.

I felt the momentum building and the groove started to include Will. We fed off each other's energy and started to function as a unit. I felt like a passenger and the ice was a magic carpet.

A breath over three hours from the car, we clipped the top anchor. I grabbed the rap ropes Will had organized while he belayed. Just over four hours from starting out we were back at the truck, gorging ourselves on turkey, apple turnovers, and Red Bull™. We'd climbed Polar Circus an hour faster than my muddled solo the year before.

By the time we reached the bottom of the Weeping Pillar, I was very much ready to jump on the sharp end. Spending the early morning in the backseat had given me enough time to get centered, find the right pace, and relax. Now I was ready to take the wheel and drive for a while.

I reached the first belay behind the central pillar, put Will on belay, and stuffed my face with gel and water while he climbed. Pull in the rope, squeeze some gel, slosh some water. Pull in the rope, squeeze some gel, slosh some water. When Will stopped to clean a screw, I took a few extra seconds to get organized for the next pitch. He appeared around the pillar with the gear already coming off his shoulder.

Laugh, nod and smile, on belay, go.

We functioned as an upward-motion machine, smoothly switching from leader to second, second to leader. The more energy we put into the endeavor, the more our partner received and returned. We finished the first half of the Weeping Pillar almost two hours ahead of schedule. My anal mind noted that we averaged four screws and 25 minutes per pitch. While I tallied statistics, Will bounded ahead toward his last block.

As we marched across the halfway ledge, I noticed a growing stiffness in my right wrist. The tendon that is so crucial for drawing back an ice tool was getting aggravated. I later found out that it's a common overuse injury in carpenters. I mentioned it to Will; he said that he felt a bit of the same.

On the upper wall, the beaming sunlight felt good, but it threatened our safety. We shed our outer layers and continued up in clothing more common to summer sidewalk coffee shops. As we delaminated, so did the ice.

"How much rope left?" Will yelled, 900 feet above the highway.

"80 feet!" I estimated. It was an unlikely question for Will to ask, so I assumed that the pitch was harder, longer, or steeper than it looked. By the time I seconded it, Will's screws had melted out; they took only a few turns and a hard yank to remove. The ice was steep, funky, and soft—fun to top-rope, engaging to lead. As I clipped in to the belay, Will apologized for taking so long.

"Relax," I said. He'd climbed a healthy, 70-meter dose of WI 6 in 25 minutes.

We were on top of the Weeping Pillar by noon. A confident smile started to creep across my face. In 1980, James Blench and Albi Sole set a new, steep-ice standard by climbing the Weeping Pillar in over two days. Modern methods allow most climbers to do the route, similar to Polar Circus, in 10 to 12 hours. An hour's rappel would put us back at the car in less than five, but a growing pain in my wrist reminded me that the fat lady hadn't sung.

Due to fatigue and overconfidence, I foolishly rapped past icicles that I should have kicked off. I cursed myself as I got to the ledge and looked up into a dripping, 1000-pound spear. I cowered under a rock outcrop while Will encouraged hundreds of pounds of ice to roar to the halfway ledge 600 feet below.

The drive over to Curtain Call did not help my confidence. Originally climbed by Jeff Lowe and Mike Weis in 1979, Curtain Call is often described as "one of the scariest routes around." It forms every year—often as a narrow, 70-foot totem—and may or may not get an ascent before it collapses under its own weight. Despite getting a half hour to eat some real food and rehydrate, the extra time was enough for my tendon to start creaking in its sheath. Changing my socks and retying my boots was a painful, gritted-teeth affair.

The approach revealed our newfound relaxation—or the critical mass of our fatigue. It was early afternoon and Curtain Call wouldn't take more than a couple hours. With the end of the tunnel in plain, sunlit view, we slowed down. As we plodded upward, I grabbed handfuls of snow and pressed them into my wrist.

Drained and inattentive, I chose a time-consuming line instead of a more expedient one. Involuntary grunts became regular accompaniment for each swing. I continued up, battling with steep mushrooms and a hand that had a mind of its own. I placed too many screws and climbed straight through a cold, dripping shower. Already starting to worry about the next pitch, I put in my last screw for a belay, buried my axes, and started to bring Will up.

The cool thing about that moment was that I found myself in one of the best belay spots in the world; I could have hosted a 20-person dance party on that ledge. The sky was a comforting, bluebird dome and the sun had come around enough to sparkle in liquid drips.

As he calmly pulled through the shower, Will saw the epic I was having just pulling rope through the belay device. I knew that venturing out onto the sharp end for my last pitch would have been slow, stupid, and dangerous. I wanted to finish my block, but it would have cost us time with excess screws and pain-reduced speed.

"Do you wanna bail?" asked Will. Positions reversed, I hoped I would have asked him the same thing.

"Fuck that," ricocheted inside my skull. I handed him the last sling and grabbed his pack. Will fired the last pitch, while I grunted and groaned my way up it. My right arm was useless as I pulled over the lip. Dummy arm without a pump. Nod and smile, a left-handed high five.

Two quick, painful raps and we were on the ground heading for the road like horses for the barn. A burst of energy accompanied the thrill of being done—and done so quickly. Will threw his gear into a tangled jumble in the back of the truck and tossed me a Red Bull™. I smiled and pitched my gear onto the pile. I thought about sorting it out, but for once the cluster didn't matter.

— Scott Semple

CHAPTER 6

Guy Lacelle on a new route in Quebec, Canada. (Photo © Will Gadd)

Advanced Ice Technique

My favorite ice climbs offer the least-possible-looking lines: thin pillars stretching up into space, 2-inch-thick smears, and wild combinations of ice that defy gravity and almost beg a climber, "Come on, let's see what you can do with this!" Advancements in gear, protection, and climbing skill have all contributed to the variety of ice terrain we can now climb with some degree of safety.

TECHNIQUES FOR STEEP ICE CLIMBING

The steeper ice becomes, the wilder and more engaging the climbing gets. Ice seldom forms in continuous overhangs, but danglers, large spray cones, and other unusual situations often produce short overhanging sections. Even truly vertical ice often feels overhanging because your tools and crampons force you out away from the ice. Each time you move on ice—steep or otherwise—be sure to move into balance first so that the foot or tool you want to move is unweighted. "Hopping" your foot on ice seldom works well, and frequently leads to both feet blowing. You can often achieve momentary balance by pushing down (with your hand still in the leash or on the bottom grip); this might seem awkward at first, but using your tools to both push and pull helps you to stay balanced and smooth.

The trick for climbing steep ice is to move efficiently between rests, protect before the climbing gets really hard, and use every trick you can think of to make things relatively easy and safe. On long, vertical pitches there still almost always will be good places to rest, either on bumps in the ice or in shallow grooves. I have yet to find a true pitch of dead vertical ice with absolutely no place to take the majority of

Even "overhanging" ice can often be stemmed around.

An open mind leads to good movement.

weight off your hands—if you know the moves. Most of the good steep ice tricks come from rock climbing, so I use the standard terms for the moves in the following.

Backsteps. In general you always want to have two solid feet every time you move a tool, but sometimes it's good to do a backstep or outside edge to make a long reach. Remember to make the low foot very solid; if it blows, you'll shock-load the high tool heavily.

Grooves. The best ice and best rests are often found in grooves; stemming, drop knees, and even chimneying all work well.

The goal is always to reduce the amount of weight on your arms. (See previous page)

Rock-on rests. It's possible to rest on a protrusion as small as two inches if you know how to rock on.

Sidepulls allow the climber to reach farther laterally than normally possible. Be sure to set the pick for the sidepull not a straight-down pull.

Leg hooks often work well as an alternative to heel spurs. I prefer soft-shell fabric on my legs partially for this reason.

Heel hooks work great for pulling over roofs, staying centered on small columns, and climbing off-axis pillars. Big heel spurs,

Ice climbing is a full-contact sport. Leg hooks can be very good.

Heel hooking can provide crucial balance on pillars.

A classic sidepull

such as those found on bolt-on crampons for mixed routes, get in the way too much for walking, so most climbers don't use them, but a small screw set in the bail of the crampon works well for basic heel hooks on pure ice.

Ice underclings and sidepulls allow climbers to reach out across broken-off pillars and often make a desperate move reasonable.

Cross-throughs. Leashless tools reduce the need to cross through as often, but crossing through is still often faster and more secure than matching. The ability to swing a tool in a crossed position is essential but difficult to develop. I'll often practice by climbing an entire pitch, crossing up my swings on every move.

Confidence is everything on steep terrain, and I gain confidence by visualizing

Crossing through is often the best way to move up on small pieces of ice.

how I'll climb the line until I can really see each change in pitch, move, and protection point. I'll go so far as to mime the moves on the ground that I expect to find on the pitch; this may look silly, but it works extremely well.

THIN ICE

There's nothing more rewarding than cleanly dancing your way up a wild smear of thin ice. Thin ice is a challenging medium; it is seldom consistent from day to day or even hour to hour, as temperature swings affect it drastically. What is well bonded to the rock in the morning can be worthless as the afternoon sun melts it, then fine again the next morning as the water refreezes. These changes can occur even midroute with startling speed—there's nothing worse than being halfway up a pitch and realizing that it's all delaminating and you're standing on plates of ice that just aren't going to be there much longer. If the water source ends and the temperature remains cold, the ice will hang in there for a while but eventually dry out, detach, and become miserable to climb. My favorite days for climbing thin ice occur when the temperature has been between –19 and –16° C (-2– +3° F) for at least a full day; the ice will be relatively plastic but still attached.

THIN ICE TECHNIQUE

Thin ice climbing demands a certain lightness of skating attitude. On very thin ice a blown tool or foot may result in a less

Tenuous, scary, and yet somehow very enjoyable

than enjoyable fall. The key is to move slowly and carefully, with a high degree of awareness about how your movement is affecting each placement. First of all, stop swinging with anything but your wrist. If the ice is thinner than about 3 inches, a hard swing will just blow it up like so much glass—and wreck your pick. Look very carefully at the ice before swinging; small deposits of ice that have built up on edges ("eyebrows"), mini-ice "eggs," and especially the backs of corners or the backs of larger ledges often offer two or three times as much ice as that found on a pure slab. Any place where the ice can bond with two or more surfaces (corners and grooves) will produce much more solid and often slightly thicker ice. In general, it's best to use a short, light pecking motion, gently hitting the same spot repeatedly until the tool is as deep as it's going to get. If you keep hitting at it, once the pick is close to the rock you'll blow the rock/ice bond apart and ruin the placement.

I like to use a pulling-down motion at the end of each very short swing; this tends to set the pick and displace less ice. On extremely thin ice I sometimes chip a small edge for my pick and then use the edge with my pick turned sideways to reduce the shear potential. Another useful trick is to place your pick on the ice, then pull down with a hard jerk. If your pick is sharp it will cut into the ice until it stops; repeat this motion a few times and eventually you will have a good notch scraped into the ice for your pick. Also try repeatedly and lightly tapping the head of one tool into the ice with your other tool; this bizarre-sounding trick often works well when nothing else will. This is an unstable position for your pick, but it works if you are gentle and smooth. Very thin ice climbing often becomes much like drytooling (see the "Drytooling" section in Chapter 8, Mixed

Tap, Tap, Gentle!

Ice "eyebrows" are often the best placements.

Half snow, half-ice: Use with care.

Climbing), only using ice edges that you create or find rather than rock. The same rules apply: keep the tool very steady and the angle of pull constant.

Footwork becomes even more critical when your tool placements won't hold the shock if your feet blow. Try to use the placements your tools created with your feet—you know they're solid. If you can, keep your feet very stable as you move, then they won't blow off. Keep the force on your feet straight down, rather than leaning into the ice and pushing your feet off. I sometimes find it useful to chip small edges in the ice for the crampons. Very light, delicate, and repeated kicks or even

scratches will create a drytool-style edge for your feet.

Perhaps the worst ice of all is what the Europeans call *verglass*, often found on alpine climbs in the morning when meltwater has frozen during the night. This ice isn't secure enough to hold anything but still makes the rock incredibly slippery. The line between thin ice and *verglass* can be blurry; try playing on a top-rope to figure out the absolute limitations of what your tools will hold in. This is really fun, especially on steep terrain, and you'll be thankful for the experience when the real deal shows up on your lead.

THIN ICE PROTECTION

Unfortunately, good protection on thin ice is often an oxymoron; rock gear is usually the only solution on really thin ice, but very short ice screws and ice hooks have helped open up the possibilities in recent years. I have done routes such as the Replicant in early season conditions that simply will not take any screw longer than about 13cm in the whole pitch, but the ice can be good enough that the climber feels secure both due to the placements and protection. Look for ice eyebrows and other slightly thicker areas to place screws. It's also common to sling icicles and small pillars; these are often the best and fastest form of protection on thin routes.

If the climb is detached, it may be possible to punch in two holes relatively far apart and run a sling behind a more solid piece of the climb—this is a desperate measure. Ice hooks also seem promising on detached ice, but again they are a desperate measure. Pound them into icy cracks, however, and they can be bomber!

Thin ice climbs are often basically done as solos while dragging a rope. If the ice is well attached and you feel very solid, this is perhaps reasonable, but don't let the fact that a rope is hanging off your harness influence your style of climbing. Be smooth and solid and back off while backing off is possible!

CLIMBING EARLY SEASON ICE

Early season, or "new," ice (see the "Ice Formation: Understanding the Medium" section in Chapter 3, Basic Ice Climbing) is often little more than unconsolidated icicles stuck together with the climber's optimism. This type of terrain is difficult to protect and hard to climb with any security—a worrisome combination—but I love the feeling of climbing absolutely fresh early season climbs. I try to look beyond the icicles and see the situation more as a thin ice route obscured with removable obstacles. Clearing the icicles is a major chore; be extra careful with the longer ones, which tend to fracture into pieces that rain down long after you think it's safe to look up. Try to take the major icicles down in small pieces while ducking your head. Look for good placements and protection in the thicker and more uniform ice where the icicles reconnect to the rock and just above where they dripped off. All the thin ice rules apply.

Some icicles may be very solid if climbed with the hands. For maximum security, grab them either close to where they dripped off the rock or to where they reattach. Some climbers like woolen mitts for this reason. If the icicle or glove is damp, it will freeze to the ice and be even more solid. I personally find wool mitts a pain; fleece gloves work well enough most of the time. Also try hooking your elbow around larger icicles to take the strain off your hands.

Hooking icicles with your tools also works well. Icicles can be incredibly strong if the pressure is applied slowly and near the point of origin as a lieback hold. I often see climbers trying to get a stick into an eight-inch icicle; it's usually better just to hook it. For security I'll sometimes move my tool back and forth with a sawing action before it's hooking the icicle; this creates a shallow groove in which to seat the tool better.

Footwork is tricky on these routes: be very delicate and treat your foot placements as though they were drytool edges for best results. If you have to place a crampon directly into an icicle, try to gently kick it as high up as possible; this is where the icicle will be the most solid.

DEALING WITH SUNBAKED ICE

Sunbaked ice is one of those spring nightmares of passage. I've seen up to a foot of loose "sugar ice" on the upper Weeping Wall and other sun-afflicted routes. If the ice is thick, a serious digging expedition is usually the only way to unearth a good, solid stick. On top-rope it's possible to just run up the outer layer on easy, soft sticks, but this is a good way to fall off on lead. It's not uncommon to take an hour or more on a difficult sunbaked-ice lead. Be extra careful to build really solid pockets for your feet; I find sunbaked ice far less predictable for my feet than normal ice. What feels solid by normal standards may not be.

If the baked ice is thin, you're going to have to trust whatever ice there is or retreat. Try to set deep hooks with repeated lighter swings, then firmly set each hook by yanking down hard on the tool. If the tool takes this amount of force, it will hold your weight as long as your feet don't blow. Be sure to move slowly and with a constant pull on the placement, much as you would while drytooling.

Getting good protection on baked ice may require excavating a foot-square hole. A screw in sunbaked ice is nearly worthless, but often good ice is in there somewhere.

FREE-HANGING AND FREESTANDING ICE

Climbing any free-hanging or free-dangling "stalactite ice" obviously ups the risk factor, but we all do it, so here's how to climb them. First of all, almost all free-hanging or freestanding ice falls down not when the temperature rises as one might expect but during a cold snap. The amazing pillar on Curtain Call in the Canadian Rockies often falls down during the first −34°C (−29°F) arctic cold front of the season. I have climbed numerous pillars and free-hanging icicles relatively early in the season, only to come back a few weeks later after a big drop in tem-

perature to find them lying in pieces on the ground.

Most large (over about 50 feet in length) freestanding or free-hanging ice starts out as water running off the lip of a large drop. Ice forms on the lip and over the spraying water, often in fantastic combinations, before encasing the falling water in an ever-lengthening free-hanging ice tube. This type of higher-water-volume hanging ice is generally not very stable to climb on; the water may move around irregularly, and the spray often forms very unbalanced, large hanging ice masses. This is perhaps the most dangerous type of free-hanging ice to climb. The water falls out of the tube into the air, sprays and scatters, and then forms a relatively large spray cone at the bottom. Eventually the ice tube/icicle mess and the spray cone may join to form a pillar: the Fang and Pilsner Pillar are classic examples of high-flow pillar formation. At first this pillar will be quite unstable, but with time the water tends to fill in the gaps between icicles and even out, producing a very stable tube of ice. If you ever find the remnants of a large pillar or stalactite on the ground, take a look at the crosssection; unlike trees, which form in concentric rings, big pillars form as thousands of icicles, which slowly cement together.

Eventually the tube in the middle of the pillar ices up and the water spills out over the top in a new path, increasing the size and solidity of the pillar as long as there is a constant supply of water (picture a small drainage culvert in winter—often it freezes up and floods the road). However, if the supply of water stops, the pillar will start to dry out and lose structural integrity. I like to think of ice as acting something like a sponge; if the temperature remains below freezing, it will absorb water until it reaches saturation and starts creating new ice or it will dry out and become a weak husk of its former self. Very dry ice is unstable, and very warm ice is also unstable.

Most really dramatic, skinny pillars and stalactites are shorter (less than 50 feet) and form more gradually with smaller amounts of consistent water building them up from the outside—the same process that forms icicles on your house. A smaller and generally denser spray cone also forms as the water drips off the end of the icicle, and if the slow supply of water is constant, eventually the cone and stalactite will link into a pillar. Pillars and stalactites that form very slowly in this manner tend to be quite dense and solid if the supply of water is steady. Often a promising dangler will never reach the ground even if it remains damp; at a certain point the mass of the ice seems to reach a balance with the very slow trickle of water and the feature will cease to grow but remain solid.

Judging the solidity of pillars is an art. In general, if the pillar is larger than about two meters in width, is old enough to have filled in nicely, and is very well connected to a solid-seeming older spray cone at the bottom, it is safe to climb. If the primary support for the pillar appears to be its attachment point at the top, it probably isn't safe and should be treated as a stalactite. I have climbed many pillars only

to find a three- to six-inch crack that seemingly runs all the way through the pillar near the top; this used to freak me out until I realized that my weight was pretty minor compared to the weight of the pillar and that almost invariably the core of the pillar had refrozen the two sections together. The Fang, Pilsner Pillar, and many other climbs often have this crack but seldom fall down until spring.

Climbers will sometimes hang an old rope or even steel cable down a promising water drop to help a pillar form. This seems to help the formation, but no rope or cable is strong enough to actually support a large pillar. I have seen half-inch steel cable snapped like twine from the weight of the ice.

Ice is very good at supporting its own weight from below but very fragile when that weight is hanging—the bond is under a lot of tension. Judging the solidity of free-hanging ice is a serious game, and plenty of good climbers have been injured or even killed by guessing wrong. But of course, we keep guessing and going for it, so here's how I approach the experience.

What keeps the dangling ice from falling off? Primarily the strength of the bond between the ice and the rock, with perhaps additional support from the tensile strength of the curved ice on the lip. This bond can be very strong (think of how difficult it is to chip ice off a cold sidewalk or how long an icicle can get from the roof of a house relative to the surface area at the top), but it is always suspect. I have found a few rough rules of thumb helpful for what should be understood as a guessing game at best.

- Note how ridiculous the potential climb looks. If the ice is hanging down more than about four times the diameter of its attachment point (40-foot dangler from a 10-foot-diameter attachment point), it's probably very unstable.
- Climbing danglers in cold weather is a bad idea. It's hard to get your picks in, and the whole feature is generally much more brittle if you hit it too hard.
- Look at the shape of the stalactite. If it's round and well attached all the way around its circumference (and you can see this attachment to make this guess), that's a plus.
- If the ice is early stage and very chandeliered, it's probably less stable and much more difficult to climb securely.
- Look at the shape of the feature. Curtains, or horizontal features, tend to fracture much more easily under a climber's weight than cylinders do.
- Examine how much mass is seemingly forward of the lip and how much is seemingly behind the lip. The perfect free-hanger would be completely bonded around its circumference and then get quickly narrower below it. If the hanger looks unbalanced or has formed off-axis, it's probably very unstable. Many of the pillars in Ouray are unstable because they form from a "shower nozzle" spraying water out past the lip, resulting in a hanger with most of its mass forward of the attachment point.

Nothing is more attractive and stylish than climbing a large icicle in some form, but climbing this type of terrain is full of risks even for those who have climbed a lot of it. Here are some "rules" to live by.

- Anchor the belayer well off to the side, completely out of the way even if the whole rig falls down. An unanchored belayer will often get pulled into the impact zone if the leader falls, and whacking your belayer is bad form at best.
- Place gear off to the side of the hanger in the rock and as high as possible so that if all hell breaks loose, you will swing safely off to the side. If you don't have gear to the side and the ice breaks, even very small features can kill you.
- Keep the rope organized. Wild, three-dimensional gyrations are common when getting on hangers from the rock, but if the rope gets twisted around your body or neck, the fall can be really nasty—you violently unspin with the rope like a human top.
- Never, never put protection into anything that you are even moderately concerned about breaking. I see many leaders placing screws in unstable features—this is dangerous. If they break, you go for a ride—attached to 'em. If you don't feel you can climb the feature without the security of ice screws, don't climb it.
- Know that most delicate pieces of ice break near their attachment points, so don't think you're safe because the feature is getting thicker! The ice is under the greatest tension and load near the attachment point; even very large hangers can break at or near their

attachment points from a light swing. Only place gear, swing hard, or celebrate when both tools are well above the attachment point to the rock. Many climbers treat the bottom of the icicle as the crux. Although the start is often the most technically demanding, the last few feet before the rock, even if the ice sounds solid, are usually the most dangerous.

- On very thin hangers, don't swing. File your picks mercilessly until they can scratch down the surface of the ice and catch. Use small holes, spaces between icicles, and air pockets as holds rather than creating placements. This reduces impact forces. Don't kick. Use very sharp crampons and climb the feature as if it was rock. If you must create something to stand on, then slide your points down until they catch.

- Climb thin features when the temperature has just risen or when the sun has just hit the feature. This softens the surface, which makes getting solid but very delicate sticks easier.

- If the stalactite is dangling down to within reach of your tool, it's best to start with a solid hook placement and then go immediately into a figure four. The other option is doing one-arm pull-ups. After both tools are in, ice heel spurs are very useful for upward progress.

- Be very careful kicking the ice down low; it tends to break off. (Note that the whole hanger doesn't usually break; there's generally still enough flex low to keep the whole mass from breaking off.)

SUFFER MACHINE FALL

It was the fall of 1997 and I had been climbing a lot—climbing lots of free-hangers, too—Auto de Feu, Burning Man. . . . It all combined to lull me into a false sense of security, into feeling that I was in complete control.

Rumor had it that Dave Thomson had put up an M8 on the Stanley Headwall—Teddy Bear's Picnic—the direct start to the unformed pillar of Suffer Machine. I had no clue about M grades, but an eight sounded exciting. I had to have a go at it.

The morning of December 1 found Dave Campbell and me hiking up to the headwall. There was little snow, but it was cold, at least −12°C. The plan was to quickly fire the first pitch of Suffer Machine, then rap off and move on to the four-pitch Uniform Queen. We geared up and scrambled a few meters up to the belay ledge, from where a friendly line of bolts led up to the huge hanging dagger.

Right from the start the drytooling was overhanging, but tool placements were bomber and I was clipping a bolt every second move. Below a small horizontal roof I paused to rest. A piece of tat hung from the last bolt, after which the route went onto the dagger. I clipped the tat, leaned out, and felt over the roof. Nothing here, blank rock there, but here was a good edge. I released the lower tool and swung backhanded into the ice hanging in space behind my head. I got a good hook and swung my feet across.

The ice was lacy and aerated, and my monos kept shearing through. I climbed into a no-hands rest between the rock and the ice. After a while I started up again. Above where the ice attached to the back wall, I placed a screw. A few meters higher I placed another to protect the moves onto the front of the curtain. Once around to the front, I looked up to see smooth ice quickly easing in angle. I started placing my tools more forcefully. Then there was a dry crack and my stationary world blurred into free fall.

I fell for a long time, long enough for thought. There was the sound and fury of ice breaking up around me, and then all was quiet. I was hanging at the end of the ropes, a few meters below the belay and a couple meters above the ground. My crampons were dangling from my boots by their straps; one of my tools was some way down the slope. The screws I had placed were hanging on the ropes in front of me, with Screamers™ still intact. I felt no pain but instinctively knew I had to get out to the road before whatever I had done to my body caught up with me. But pride insisted that we pull and coil the ropes. It was a controlled retreat, not a rout. On both ropes the core was exposed 12 meters from the ends, where they had abraded against the edge of the roof. With rope stretch, I must have fallen at least 25 meters. Looking up, I could see that the curtain had fractured across its entire width far above where it had appeared to attach to the rock.

By the time we pulled into Canmore, I was so stiff I could barely climb out of the car and hobble into the hospital. The immediate diagnosis was that nothing was broken. It later turned out that I had damaged nerves in my right arm. It was a few months before I regained sensation and full motor function. But I always knew I would climb again. Two weeks after the accident I scrambled up Mount Rundle with my arm in a sling. Another two weeks elapsed and I tried leading Wicked Wanda. Having almost no control over my right arm made placements difficult, and I realized my mind would have to give my body time to catch up.

These days I will still get out on free- hangers, but I am much more aware of my surroundings. I gauge the temperature, listen to the hollow noises made by the dagger, and try to be as gentle as possible, even where the ice already appears to attach to the rock. But above all I realize that being in complete control, being able to precisely predict my impact on the ice, is only an illusion. I try to act accordingly.

— Raphael Slawinski

CHAPTER 7

Will Gadd on "Call of the Curtain," Icefield Parkway, Jasper National Park, Canada

Leading and Protecting Mixed Routes

You know, all this gear is mostly for show anyhow. Real security comes from not falling off.

> — *Jeff Lowe, after a new*
> *route in Colorado*

There are few more satisfying experiences than leading a traditional (nonbolted) mixed pitch safely and in control. There are few more terrifying experiences than leading a mixed pitch out of control and fearing that at any second it's all going to go bad. Traditional mixed climbing requires a very complete set of skills: the ability to judge a climb's character and your own temperament, as well as place ice and rock gear and be creative in mixing all of these games together. Traditional mixed climbing requires a strong head, meaning that the leader can make good judgments about how secure she is, how good the gear is, and what will happen as she climbs higher. I've backed off more mixed pitches than I can remember, yet there are still those leads I wish I'd backed off of earlier. Be careful; realize that the gear is often difficult to get and not as solid. I'm a believer in running away often so I can come back and climb another day; no route is worth a bad injury.

Traditional mixed leads can go very quickly if the cracks are ice-free and the ice is well bonded, but more often than not they take time if they are to be done safely. I find that I move faster on difficult ground if I have good gear; taking time to put in the gear may actually be faster than sketching your way up some thin seam 40 feet above questionable gear!

PROTECTION

Most mixed climbs feature bolted rock sections connecting one or more ice sections. On harder routes the rock protection tends to be bolts; often the rock on mixed climbs is so poor that even a good nut is questionable. If you're climbing a new route from the ground up on natural gear, plan your protection points from the ground and take an appropriate rack. Pitons are often the only viable option for iced-up cracks (see the "Thin Ice Protection" section in Chapter 6, Advanced Ice Technique, for more information).

THE RACK

Mixed routes often demand larger racks, especially if the climb is difficult. On easier mixed routes I'll usually take the following:

4–6 ice screws: 1 long for V-threads, 1–2 medium length, and 2 stubbies

6 nuts: across the range

2 Tricams: .5 and 1

1 hex: larger (7– 9 or so)

2–3 cams: blue Metolius™, maybe a red and yellow Camalot™

6 pitons: 3 blades, 3 angles

1 V-thread hooker

6–7 slings

10 free carabiners on the above slings

3 locking carabiners

2 cordelettes

For more serious routes, I'll often end up with a much larger rack. Make the second carry whatever the leader doesn't want, or leave it on the ground at the base of the route. A common rack for a bigger one-day mixed route might consist of the following:

10–12 ice screws: normal rack, because there may be one or two full pitches of ice

10 nuts: full range of stoppers from $3/8$ inch to 1 inch

2 Tricams: .5 and 1

1 hex: #9

cams: a full set of smaller cams (4 that

work from about $^1/_4$ to 1 inch), plus a full set of cams up to $3^1/_2$ inches. For granite, take 2 red Camalots™ or equivalent; they seem to be "the" piece.

12 pitons: For limestone, take 6–8 blades and the rest angles; for granite, take 4 blades, 4 Lost Arrows/Bugaboos™, 4 angles

10 slings: 5 rigged as quickdraws, 5 as over shoulder

15 free carabiners

5 quickdraws

1 V-thread

2 cordelettes

3 locking carabiners

Obviously this is a lot of gear, but unless it's a multiday route you can always leave some of it at the base if things are very different from what you anticipated. If possible, talk with someone who has done the route recently to cut down on the amount of gear that you have to cart in, but don't take that advice as gospel. In general, more technical gear is not all that heavy to carry and often allows a safer, faster ascent in the long run.

Note: The following information assumes a basic familiarity with rock gear.

CAMS

I've heard all kinds of well-educated theories about cams working well in icy cracks, but almost every one I've ever jerk-tested pulled out. I've had cams even fall out under their own weight in *verglassed* or mossy cracks. For a cam to work well, both sides of the placement must be free of snow, ice, and dirt. Use your tool to aggressively remove the assorted munge; really scrape the sides of the crack to assure adequate friction. Even a very thin layer of icy moss will cause a cam to slide out easily; always jerk-test any cam. In general, if you can't get the placement perfectly clean, then assume it's not all that great. Often the best possible cam cracks are found in the walls of corners or gullies where ice hasn't accumulated; it's easy to overlook cracks and other features off to the side of the thin strip of ice you're climbing. I often use cams more as large nuts on mixed climbs; be sure your cams will work as nuts if they are fully open.

NUTS

Sometimes life is good and nuts happily slot like they're supposed to in perfect, clean flares. However, because mixed climbs are often water-worn during the summer, placements tend to be shallow or to flare awkwardly. Opposed nuts, equalized nuts, and other tricks of nut craft are essential, but sometimes a little friendly force helps fit a nut where nature didn't want it. Find a nut that almost fits, then beat on it until it's well stuck in the crack. (Try not to hit the wire or damage the surrounding rock with your hammer or pick.) If you can free both hands, keep downward tension on the nut while beating it senseless. If the placement is tenuous at first, clip the nut in to the rope; that way it will only rattle off down the rope when it falls out instead of disappearing into either space or a snowdrift at the bottom.

HEXES

Hexes are lighter than cams and often outperform them, especially on limestone and other irregular rock. They can also be pounded into place, but be careful not to overpound them and bend the tubes. I find the larger sizes most useful for replacing large cams; it's amazing how often the #9 will work on rock. Leaving a hex as a rap anchor is also a lot less financially painful than leaving a cam ($15 versus $60)! I like the open ends on the hexes; they will often catch perfectly on little rugged features in cracks and otherwise snake their way into confined areas.

I have used hexes between icicles, but I consider this is a desperate move and they probably won't hold much.

TRICAMS

Tricams (formerly known as Lowe Tricams) work well in icy, mangy, and flaring cracks. I always carry the two smallest sizes (.5–1). The unique shape seems to fit better both as a nut (not cammed) and as a passive (no springs; the load cams the nut) placement in the weird cracks common on mixed climbs. Be sure to set a Tricam aggressively; they lack springs to keep tension on the cam, so even a small movement may cause it to fall out. I often beat on Tricams a little bit like nuts to set them extra solidly, but be careful of the sling!

PINS

Pitons are often the best mixed climbing protection short of a 3-inch stainless bolt, but they take some experience to place competently. Find a road cut or boulder unsuitable for "real" climbing or other aesthetic pursuits, then place and remove pins until you get the hang of it. In general, the perfect pin would be difficult to drive just about as the head was reached and it would make a singing sound for the last few hits. Pins that stick out should be tied off; often the end of a quickdraw works well or it can be tied off. An afternoon spent pounding and pulling pins will teach you more about their use and feel than 2000 words, so I'll stop with that. There is nothing like pounding in and removing pins on the ground to prepare for the experience 20 feet above your last piece.

Make sure the piton crack is in solid rock and not alongside a detached block obscured by snow or ice. A pin in a less-than-solid crack generally won't start to sing as you beat on it. Clear debris out of the crack first; although pins will often displace ice or munge as they go in, steel on rock is always stronger. Once a pin stops moving in, stop pounding on it; overdriving only damages the placement and warps the pin, often enlarging the hole enough that it stops firmly holding the pin in place. If a pin goes in very easily, take it out and put in a bigger one. Many munge placements will take several pitons of increasing thickness before finally ringing solidly. Angles are often more reliable than blades or Lost Arrows™ because they have three points of contact—I've had fewer good angles pull out than supposedly bomber blades. However, blades often work better in limestone than anything else. Baby angles are universally great.

When you encounter a fixed pin on a mixed climb, generally assume it's garbage. The radical freeze/thaw action on mixed routes, combined with rust and time, makes even the most solid pin deteriorate quickly. Give the suspect pin a light tap with your hammer; if it rings, clip it and go. If it doesn't ring gently, give it a harder tap to see if you can reseat it. If that fails, pull it out and put in a good pin.

ICE HOOKS

Note: I exclusively use Spectres™ from Black Diamond. They are heavy but last a long time and take a tremendous amount of abuse. Hooks from other manufacturers may be lighter, but lighter generally equals less resistance to abuse. As with all gear, try out the competing brands and make your own final decision.

Most people think of Spectres™ and other hooks as ice gear, but my experience is that unless they're perfectly placed in perfect ice and loaded very smoothly straight down, then either the hook breaks the ice or, more often, falls out from rope movement or the outward force of a fall. However, Spectres™ are often the only gear that will work well in mungy cracks, frozen moss, and other unorthodox situations. I've fallen enough on Spectres™ to have faith in their holding power. Experiment on the ground; getting a welded Spectre out takes some experience, but after seeing how well they work in even ridiculous situations, you'll probably be more trusting of a well-bashed Spectre.

Many climbs have frozen munge ledges—"munge" meaning some combination of grass, dirt, ice, and rocks frozen together like Rocky Road ice cream. I've found a Spectre useful in this situation; just hammer it in to the hilt. If there's a lot of resistance and the Spectre starts ringing, it's probably good. A pick hole helps to start a Spectre in this situation.

If you do have to use a Spectre in ice, try holding it in place with a stubby screw or nut below it and equalizing the two so that the stubby keeps it in place. (Don't place the screw too close to the Spectre, and be sure to extend the placement with a sling to reduce rope drag and outward force.)

MIXING PRO

Many mixed climbs require mixing different styles of protection. For example, a shallow nut may be great for a downward pull but nearly worthless for an outward pull. Even a relatively poor screw placed appropriately can help the nut resist an outward pull from rope movement or the initial outward force of a fall. An "okay" stubby equalized with a tied-off icicle works well too, but be sure to use a cordelette-style equalization system rather than a twisted sling. If tying off an icicle doesn't offer good protection by itself, place a Spectre or stubby and equalize the two. I often end up with as many as four pieces of equalized gear for one protection point.

An I-thread (rather than a V-thread) may offer surprisingly good protection when nothing else will work.

CREATIVE SLING USAGE

If you keep your eyes open and use your V-thread creatively, it's often possible to tie off frozen-in blocks or thread chockstones, roots, or whatever. One of my favorite mixed climbing tricks is to tie off on a big rock fin or thin block that's frozen into the ice in the back of a groove. Give potential blocks a good, solid whack with your hammer at the point farthest from the ice; if it holds that, it may be extremely solid. Frozen-in blocks can often be slung by chipping a nice groove around their bases in the ice. Frozen-up talus may not offer enough ice for a proper V-thread, but look around the block for areas where the ice has pooled between two well-frozen touching rocks. Sometimes you can punch a quick hole with your V-thread between the blocks or just thread the existing hole. The resulting protection can be incredibly strong. Many leaders focus too much on how the ice and munge is ruining the possibilities for traditional gear rather than seeing the possibilities it opens up.

The best mixed leaders get good gear where none appears to exist—get creative!

ROPE MANAGEMENT

As you're climbing, make sure the rope doesn't snag behind loose blocks, large icicles, or other movable features (or a sharp edge). This may mean placing pro just to keep the rope organized. It's also important to protect your second from bad pendulums.

Anytime you're traversing a lot, think of your second following the pitch and place good gear just after the cruxes as you would for yourself just before the cruxes.

Finally, keep the belayer out of the line of fire; even great gear requires a functioning belayer!

BOLTS

Bolting is the hidden secret of modern mixed climbing; they just appear, and we all clip 'em with the assumption that whoever put the bolts in knew exactly what they were doing. The reality is that those bolts were probably put in by someone like me—who didn't exactly take a structural engineering course on the whole process—or you. So how good are they? Like ice screws, this is a guess. Good bolts are at least $3/8$ inch in diameter, made of stainless steel, and not rusty. It's impossible to tell how long a placed bolt is, but it should be at least 3 inches long to be really solid in all rock. A bolt is only as good as the hanger. There are a lot of nasty old hangers out there, and I've had more hangers than bolts fail on mixed and ice routes. Never hit a hanger or bolt to see if it is solid; give it a light torque with your tool if it looks suspect (smaller than $3/8$ inch; less than bomber-looking hanger) instead. If you're climbing in a bolted area, consider bringing a $1/2$-inch wrench along to tighten bolts; loose hangers are weaker.

Stick clips are appearing in bolted areas. The level of the ground may fluctuate

Stick clipping is increasingly common in mixed areas.

radically from year to year given the snowpack, and a stick clip may be the only safe solution if the first bolt is 15 feet above what was four feet of snow-covered talus but is now just talus.

If you decide to go bolting, make sure to use at least a $3^1/2$-inch stainless-steel bolt with a good hanger. Place the bolts in such a way that they will be visible if the ice moves around, as it commonly does, and consider not bolting routes that will form only once every 10 years. Place the bolts into solid features and at right angles to the rock. A power drill is the only way to go; hand-drilling often produces poor-quality, substandard holes. This type of bolt will have to be replaced eventually, and bolt scars are ugly, so do it right the first time.

As to the ethics of where to bolt and why, let the potential quality of the route, respect for your fellow climbers, and community consideration be your guides. Talk over a proposed route with other active climbers and get a feel for what they think. If I think a bolted route that I put up will get a lot of traffic and create some fun for the community, then I'll bolt it. If it's going to be an exercise in ego-stroking at the expense of the local community's ethics, I'll head somewhere else. There are a lot of great mixed routes to do; the world doesn't need another low-quality one. Do your best to think the situation through carefully; bolted routes can be great fun but not every line needs to be bolted!

CHAPTER 8

Will Gadd on "Power to Burn," Canadian Rockies

Mixed Climbing

Modern mixed climbing opens up a lot of exciting terrain. Hanging icicles, monster roofs, unformed ice climbs, and anything that's cold enough to freeze is suddenly possible. Just as sport climbing turned many formerly overlooked cliffs into destination climbing areas, modern mixed climbing has really expanded the world of winter climbing. The magazines are giving modern mixed climbing a lot of press because of the wild situations, but the game isn't new—traditional mixed climbing is one of the older, most classic forms of climbing. Paintings from over 100 years ago show wool-clad climbers with one foot on the rock and the other on ice, valiantly battling upward with a 5-foot alpenstock. Pictures from Chamonix from the 1960s to the 1990s often show a lone climber, high on a mixed alpine face. And pictures from the 1950s to the present show bold climbers scraping tenuously up one of Scotland's horrendous

"frost" climbs on Ben Nevis. So while mixed climbing today often means making radical, bolt-protected moves on steep terrain, the game has been around for a long time and offers a lot of variety.

Modern mixed climbing, often called "M-climbing" because of the M1–M12 rating system Jeff Lowe developed to rate the climbs, commonly focuses on gymnastic difficulty with relatively good preplaced protection. This should not be confused with "traditional mixed climbing," which is generally protected with lead-placed gear such as nuts and pitons. The techniques and tactics of M-climbing often work very well in the alpine environment (recent routes everywhere from the Himalaya to Canada confirm this idea), but the risk level is very different. For the rest of this discussion I'll call well-protected M-climbing "mixed climbing" and any other sort "traditional mixed climbing." Broadly, it's acceptable to fall off the well-protected sections of an M climb. Falling is in general not acceptable on a trad mixed route where the gear is usually very far apart and the angle too low to fall safely.

ETHICS

I really hate ethics discussions, as most of them are more about "My way is best and yours sucks" than any sort of real environmental or moral dilemma. That said, I've seen an increase in rock damage from mixed climbing, so here goes. Most mixed climbs are in relatively poor rock; the natural freeze/thaw cycle of water tends to fracture the rock, leaving lots of interesting edges and possible features. There is a gray area between cleaning off the loose surface rock with your pick and creating new holds; the reality is that many mixed routes require

extensive and sometimes creative cleaning, although definitely not in the same fashion as drilling pockets on a fabricated sport route. I try to do the absolute minimum of cleaning and stabilization possible, even if this means occasionally breaking a hold while climbing. There's almost always something left after a hold breaks off, but beating on a "hold" with your pick for 10 minutes to make it solid is pathetic.

Please don't drytool existing rock routes, as tempting as they may be. There are enough road cuts and obscure crags with poor rock to drytool on if you want to practice. It's just poor form to scratch up the rock on existing routes, and the additional leverage of a pick may blow holds off established rock routes that would have lasted for many years if a pry bar hadn't been inserted behind them.

Finally, if the temperature is much above freezing, don't climb routes that are held together with frozen water or mud. This "cement" will start melting, previously stable blocks can become dangerously loose, and the holds that normally would have lasted for everyone will break off.

MIXED TECHNIQUE

Mixed climbing mixes more than rock and ice. Good mixed climbers are skilled rock climbers, ice climbers, and even aid climbers. Creativity and imagination hold these three normally disparate disciplines together and allow upward progress. Developing solid skills on mixed terrain means a lot of practice; top-roping is the best way to start. Remember that many mixed climbs also have very difficult, often run-out ice climbing. The rock tends to be well protected, but you need to be solid on ice to climb a 40-foot dangling icicle with bad ground-fall potential. It's a good idea to spend at least a season climbing with more experienced mixed climbers before heading out on your own. If you're a good rock climber you'll figure out the rock part of mixed climbing, but the ice portion can still be very serious. More than one good rock climber has been badly injured falling off the ice portion of a mixed climb.

Pure mixed climbers are generally now using leashless tools or modifying their current tools for leashless climbing. You can certainly climb any mixed route out there with leashes on your tools—it's just easier and more fun with leashless tools. Many manufacturers sell add-on attachments for their standard tools; this is a good compromise if you're just getting into the game. If you are using leashed tools, be sure to remove the adzes, which often flick unerringly toward the softest thing they can find when a pick blows—the climber's head. Many climbers cover their hammers with duct tape and foam or a cut-open tennis ball.

HOW TO TELL IF A DRYTOOL PLACEMENT IS GOOD

One of the hardest skills to master in mixed climbing is "feeling" your tools. After years and years of sliding steel onto rock, I feel as though my tools are an extension of my nervous system; sometimes I swear I can feel the rock under the tip as well as if it were a handhold with bare skin. This is of course impossible, but it's a nice feeling nonetheless. Start all placements by seeing the hold, either literally or in your head. If you can see it directly then look at the solidity of the rock, how weighting the tool may make the placement more or less solid, and the expected angle of pull. If all of these factors add up to "solid," then pull lightly on the tool. Most mixed climbing is a game of smoothness: staying smooth as you transfer weight to your tools, keeping the angle of pull smooth and constant, and smoothly loading delicate placements. It's possible to move upward on a dime edge on an overhanging wall, but only if you keep the angle of pull down and not out and keep your weight centered exactly under the tip of your pick. If your feet swing out, the angle of pull will change and all bets will be off.

If you can't actually see the tool on the

rock, build a mental image of it using your tool as a blind person would a cane. Feel the tip move up onto the hold, and note if it then moves down (this means the hold is incut) or keeps moving up (an insecure upward-sloping hold) as you slide it onto the hold. It may still work if you pull straight down, but if you swing or move suddenly it will blow. Feel all over the possible hold for small edges, divots, or anything that will engage your pick more. An edge the size of a dime makes a huge difference on a gently sloping hold.

Good placements will generally engage more than just the tip of your tool. If just the pick is touching, the tool will feel "shaky." As soon as the sides of the tool or more than one tooth connect with something, the tool will feel more solid, sort of like a good stick in ice climbing.

I try to picture a cup of coffee in my hand to help visualize smooth movement: if your tool jerks, the coffee spills. Pick up a cup of coffee by the handle and practice raising it above your head, holding it out at arm's length to the side, and finally holding it down at waist level. If you can do this without spilling a drop, you're well on your way to understanding mixed climbing.

Although harder to visualize, your feet work the same way. Change the angle of push at all and they will blow, but keep that angle constant and you can climb on half of nothing all day. Rock climbers often throw their feet onto a smear and then move their ankles around dramatically with drop-knees, twists, and so on. Crampons don't smear and will skate if pushed on sideways,

so when using any tenuous feature with crampons or tools, you want to establish a direction of pull or push that works for that hold and then keep it constant.

GENERAL MOVEMENT

I try to climb with my arms as straight as possible virtually all the time. Think of your body as the pendulum of a grandfather clock: it's easier to push your weight side to side to move up than it is to just pull up. The more solid a hook or cam is, the more options you'll have for moving off of it. In general, you want to keep your head below the level of your pick, your arms relatively straight except when reaching, and your weight centered under the tool that's on the rock.

BODY TENSION AND HOLD ANGLE

A fully sloping hold can be used with your picks if you pull on it in such a way that the shaft is at roughly 90 degrees to the surface the pick is resting on. Picture half a rock-hard grapefruit stuck on a gently overhanging wall. If you just hang straight down from it with no feet, your pick will skate off its smooth surface. However, if you keep your feet on with good body tension (see Chapter 11 for exercises), you can pull down on the grapefruit fairly directly and the hold will work. To reach up off this hold, you have to maintain that tension while reaching past the hold. If the next hold is also a half-grapefruit, you have to maintain tension and pull direction as you move onto it. Often the lower pick will blow off in this situation, so you still have to maintain tension or you'll fall. This "tension" between your feet and the pick becomes more and more relevant as holds decrease in size and the angle of the climb increases.

To keep the pull constant on any hold you may have to use your heel spur as an undercling for one foot while pressing upward with the other foot. On rock this would be called a "bicycle pedal," meaning that one foot is pushing and one foot pulling. This is actually a very stable way to maintain tension. A "toe scum" is also worthwhile if you can't use your spur to pull upward on something.

The same idea applies for sidepulls and underclings that you can't Steinpull (described later in this chapter): keep the angle of pull on the pick constant through tension with your feet and you will stay on. This is a tricky concept to master, but it's essential for hard routes. If you understand it, climbing traditional mixed terrain is much more solid.

ONSIGHTING

I love to climb routes from bottom to top without falling off, and "mental maps" (see Figure 11) are my favorite tool for onsighting mixed routes. To give yourself better odds for success, thoroughly scope out all the good holds from the ground. Big horizontal cracks, big pockets, obvious incut ledges, and so on should form the main points on a mental map of the route. Relate where the bolts or protection opportunities are to these big holds; you'll probably place and clip protection from them. Also mark the potential rests. If you think you'll get a rest in only a couple of moves, you may be inspired to keep battling instead of falling.

After I have the big features, rests, and protection noted on my map, I then start looking between the main holds for smaller features that may or may not be good holds. Sometimes I picture these with question marks if I'm not sure about them. If the mixed route has been climbed, often from the ground you can figure out where others were using their picks.

Next try to carefully visualize how you will move from hold to hold, with a couple of alternate scenarios to deal with the small question marks. I often close my eyes and pantomime moving my tools, feet, and hands. Make sure you fully mentally climb the route, complete with clips, underclings, dynoes, or whatever else is required to reach the top. I use this technique on recreational climbs and for competition routes. Hard mixed routes are often so complicated that it's easy to get "lost" in the middle of them; my map and mental visualization of the route help me to move efficiently between the rests and good holds, all the way to the top.

If reality doesn't agree with your map, come up with a new plan. Don't get stuck on doing a move a certain way, but stop, look around, and make the move you can see before returning to your map. I always try to climb with an awareness of every possible hold around me in a 6-foot circle; all the features in that circle are possibly useful. When I get tired or pumped I start looking around. Often there is a rest or at least a better hold if I can just break out of my tunnel vision for a few seconds!

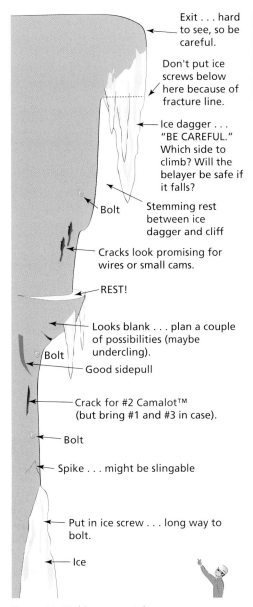

Exit . . . hard to see, so be careful.

Don't put ice screws below here because of fracture line.

Ice dagger . . . "BE CAREFUL." Which side to climb? Will the belayer be safe if it falls?

Bolt

Stemming rest between ice dagger and cliff

Cracks look promising for wires or small cams.

REST!

Looks blank . . . plan a couple of possibilities (maybe undercling).

Bolt

Good sidepull

Crack for #2 Camalot™ (but bring #1 and #3 in case).

Bolt

Spike . . . might be slingable

Put in ice screw . . . long way to bolt.

Ice

Figure 11. Making a mental map

REDPOINTING

Ah, the joy and frustration of working mixed routes! I try to onsight every route, even if it's supposedly way too hard for that. Sometimes you'll surprise yourself and do it anyhow. Most barriers to performance are mental, not physical. If you attack a route with sheer determination to succeed, no matter how hard it is, you often will. Remember that in rock climbing 5.9 was once the absolute outer limit; now first-year climbers often lead 5.11 or harder. The difference between the two eras is primarily mental. Novice climbers are not suddenly stronger than they used to be, but the perception of difficulty has changed.

Okay, so you head up in onsight mode and fail. Actually, you didn't fail; you tried and your attempt didn't work, so lose the negative attitude and decide to redpoint the rig as efficiently as possible. Before doing anything else, stop and go through what you did up to the point where you fell or whatever. That successful "mental movie" will be critical to helping you reclimb the route. Go through all the moves you can remember, how they felt, where your tools were, what move felt shaky. Once you have all that in your mind, figure out the move that rebuffed you. Most climbers fall off and start trying the move they fell on rather than taking 30 seconds to figure out what they did right up to that point: the "right" information is much more important than the "wrong" information. This brief rest also will allow you to recover some juice before climbing again.

Now work the move until you can do it,

and then keep climbing until you're starting to get pumped. Before you're totally blown out, rest and add the new section to your mental map and movie, but edit out the previous fall or sticking point. Visualize climbing from the bottom of the route to where you are now in your head. Start climbing again, repeating the process for moves that stop your upward progress until you're at the top of the route. Now you should have a complete mental map and movie of the route from bottom to top. Pull the rope, rest until you can't stand resting anymore, run around to get fully warmed up and ready to go, then send the route. You can do it. If you fall, start the process over again; repeat until you send it. Being as warm as possible before starting the route is often essential. If you're cold, you have a greater chance of injury and you will perform at a lower level.

USING YOUR HANDS

I rarely use my hands while mixed climbing. Many rock climbers moving into mixed climbing will feel secure only with their hands on the rock, but this has to be overcome. A modern mixed tool is a great hold, usually far better than any handhold on the rock. If you can crimp a hold, you can use it with your tool. If you can jam a crack with your fingers, you can cam it with your pick. On low-angle, snow-covered mixed terrain I'll use my hands to sweep off snow and grab blocks, but I've found that as my drytooling improved, my desire to use my hands fell dramatically. However, there is the occasional hold that just works better

for your hands, even with gloves on. These tend to be large bulbous holds with no positive features to set your picks on or large, smooth, downsloping ledges. Oddly, hand jams are often very solid on alpine terrain. If the terrain is steep enough that you're really hanging on a hand jam, your glove will probably pull off your hand, but on easy terrain hand jams work well.

DRYTOOLING

There are three broad types of mixed tool placement: hooks, pick cams, and tool cams.

Keep your weight low

HOOKS

Any time you use the pick of your tool on an edge it's a hook. You want to pull as straight down, or perpendicular to the edge, as possible. If you pull off to the side or out away from the pick, the pick will skate.

On most edges it's best to put the very point of your tool on the best portion of the edge. (See Photo 8-1)

Sometimes this is at the very back of the edge, sometimes on the lip, but the idea is to use the best incut feature with the point of your tool. Using the teeth farther back on the tool is seldom stable unless the edge is a fully incut jug, in which case you can do whatever you want and it will probably work.

Some edges will work best if the pick is placed parallel to the rock on the edge. (See Photo 8-2) Be careful with this placement, as any motion on the shaft will lift the pick off the edge, and the tool will tend to blow off the edge with even a minute amount of outward pull. (See Photo 8-3) I rarely use my tools sideways on edges.

Many thin cracks can have very secure hook placements in the ice or mud sitting in the crack. Even if the pick is only in one-eighth of an inch it may be very solid, but treat it as an edge rather than camming it: a cam will often just blow the placement apart. If the pick won't quite get into the ice or mud filling the crack, give the head of the tool a gentle tap; this will seat it better. Swinging at a thin crack takes a lot of precision; tapping the tool works better most of the time. Of course, if the crack is deep then cam it hard!

Bad idea. The climber is pulling out on both the tool and the pick . . .

. . . they will blow

167

Photo 8-1. A classic hook

Photo 8-2. Keep the shaft of the tool close to the rock when using the pick sidewise on an edge.

Photo 8-3. Moving the shaft out from the rock may cause the pick to skate off.

To make a long reach it's often better to choke up on the tool. (See Photo 8-4) This allows you to reach another three or four inches, but choking up also puts more outward force on the pick. On the lower grip the force is more straight down; as the climber's center of gravity moves up, the amount of outward force increases and the tool actually shifts position with the handle moving closer to the rock. (See Photo 8-4) This also often moves the contact point between the pick and the rock from the very point of the pick to several teeth back in, reducing the effectiveness of the hold. Some tools change position so radically on delicate edges that they are nearly worthless. Try out a bunch of tools with this in mind before buying any.

Rather than locking straight off when making a long reach from a thin edge, try to roll your shoulder into the rock to keep your weight under the pick and the force on the pick more downward. (See Photo 8-5) Sport climbers making the transition to mixed climbing often have a hard time remembering that changing the angle of pull on the shaft will also change the angle of pull on the pick. The key is to keep thinking about how your movement affects the angle of pull on the pick.

PICK CAMS

Parallel cracks are best climbed using various forms of pick cams. The most basic is just to stick your tool into a crack and pull sideways; as long as you keep sideways torque on the tool it's not going anywhere.

However, as soon as you relax pressure or pull straight down instead of sideways the pick will fall out. On larger cracks stick more of your pick into the crack; you should be able to cam any crack up to about an inch. Above this width you'll probably have to start camming the shaft of the tool instead of just the pick.

Photo 8-4

Photo 8-5

You can cam your picks with the shaft inverted, sideways, or whatever you can dream up. The trick is to free your imagination and have fun.

Transferring your weight from the lower tool to the higher is often a problem. As your weight comes onto the upper tool it automatically takes weight off the lower tool and puts more outward force on the lower tool. The key is to commit to your upper tool, expecting that your lower tool will release as the pressure changes, but

Keep the pull to the side of the tool for a secure pick cam.

keep your body tension high so that you don't swing off. Body tension means the ability to keep your butt from sagging and your feet from swinging off on steep terrain.

TOOL CAMS

The classic tool cam is called the "Steinpuller." Even though it doesn't really look like pulling a stein of beer on a tap, for some reason we thought it fit when we invented the word. Place the tip of your pick onto an edge or other feature under a little roof, then pull up until the head of the tool cams into the roof. (See Photos 8-7 and 8-8) The advantage of this move over just using the edge is that you can pull out or up on the tool without blowing it off the rock.

Steinpulls can be used for long upward reaches, for sidepulls, or even in a flat roof to keep your tool from falling off an edge. Each Steinpull is different, and variations abound! Teeth in the top of your pick will help prevent it from pulling out and also make the tool more stable. In photos 8-9 and 8-10, the climber takes a small pocket with her tools, then sets the top of one pick on the rock above the pocket for a Steinpull. It's important to set the Steinpull without outward pull, then add body weight, or you'll fly off the hold!

If you are reaching up to take a Steinpull, first flip the tool over in your hand so your thumb is pointed away from the pick; this technique makes the reach much easier. (See Photo 8-11)

Sometimes you can cam the entire head of your tool in wider cracks, or use the shaft

Photo 8-7. A "classic" Steinpull

Photo 8-8. An inverted Steinpull

Photo 8-9. Setting up to make a long reach off a Steinpull

Photo 8-10. Keep the pull "out" and the tool will be stable.

in the same manner (see Photo 8-12).

Stacking tools to make a long reach is a very useful technique. Most people worry that this "tool stack" places more force on the pick, but if you think about it, you're hanging on the pick anyhow so stacking doesn't really add any force.

FOOTWORK

FRONTPOINTS

Well-worn dime edges will work for your frontpoints, but only if you very precisely place your foot and then keep it totally still while you move. This concept is often the hardest part of mixed climbing for rock climbers to understand; they are used to

Photo 8-11. Flip the tool.

Photo 8-12

Stacking tools to pull up on a strenuous curtain

Monopoints often fit better in small pockets and cracks than dual points.

The possibilities are endless!
(Photo © Andrew Querner)

slapping a foot on and letting the adhesive rubber do its thing. However, if you can find a deep edge, pocket, or beat-out corner, it's possible to do all the same moves you might on rock, such as radical drop-knees. Learn to place your feet as carefully as you do your picks. Often the same edge that worked for your pick will work for your frontpoint, but it requires the same attention to placement and then keeping it still while moving upward.

HEEL HOOKS

Heel hooks are definitely the best for steep mixed climbing, especially if you have good

heel spurs bolted onto your boots. Good heel spurs open up a world of fantastic movement. Monkeys are perhaps the only other animals that can climb as steep terrain as we can with good heel spurs! A very flexible boot with bolt-on crampons works the best for mixed climbing, but even a thick plastic boot with a good heel spur will make steep terrain much friendlier. Be careful not to fall off with your heel spur well jammed, and be very careful of your legs, face, and hands while heel-hooking. I've taken several climbers to the hospital with bad heel spur injuries.

With very good heel spurs it's possible to hang almost fully upside down off both

Use a creative Steinpull to make a long reach.

spurs. We jokingly call this move "It Figures," but it does work.

MOVEMENT TRICKS

The movement in mixed climbing is often crazier and more free-form than that found in rock climbing, so be inventive and keep the sharp bits away from your soft bits. The following are some useful tricks.

THINK THREE-DIMENSIONALLY

Most climbers at first will see only the possibility for pulling straight down on a flat edge or camming in cracks. In reality, most edges are best used with the appropriate force vector, meaning they will hold a pull in only one direction better than any other. If you can learn as you do on rock, to see sidepulls, underclings, and small Steinpulls as well as flat edges you can climb a lot more routes with less effort.

Most rock climbers transitioning to mixed climbing also have to learn that instead of a 6-foot reach they really have an 8-foot-plus reach thanks to an extra 2 feet of tool in each hand. This extra reach can be very useful if exploited fully.

Daniel DuLac getting creative; tools aren't just for your hands anymore!

Photo 8-13. Setting up for a figure-4

Photo 8-14. Note how close the climber's chest is to his knee.

Releasing from a figure-four

A figure-nine

TOOL TRICKERY

A leg hook on a cammed Steinpuller tool is often very close to a total rest. The physics seem impossible, but it works really well!

On steep roofs it's often easier to hook one heel spur on your tool to clip or set up for a long reach. Hooking one pick on the shaft of the other tool is also useful for resting on large roofs.

Steep modern mixed climbing often brings out all kinds of wild contortions. If you're pumped silly, steinpull a tool and hook an elbow around it, or better yet, get a leg over it and shake out hands-free! Alternatively, rest with one or both heel spurs hooked on one tool with both hands on the other. When hanging one-armed from a tool it's often easier to get back on the rock or ice by hooking the high tool with the pick of the lower and then pulling up, like a stack on ice. There are no rules in this rapidly evolving game, just have fun and be careful when using picks and spurs close to your hands and face.

DYNOES

Dynoes are increasingly common on mixed routes. Drytool dynoes work basically the same as rock dynoes, but you can't pull out as hard on the low tool. First, scope the hold you are going for and visualize how you are going to dyno to reach it. Then get your feet up, get your arms straight, and kick hard like a frog. You can pull quite hard on the tools at first, but as your body moves higher, try to almost "mantle" the tools, only releasing the lower tool as you pass it. Look up for the hold you spotted, and fly toward it with your pick in the ready position. If the dyno is sideways or even down, as they often are now in competitions, you'll have to "catch" the finishing hold with both tools or the force will either knock your hand off the one tool or rip your shoulder apart.

FIGURE FOURS AND NINES

"Figure fours" are very useful for stabilizing in roofs and getting established on hanging ice where you can't heel-hook. They also nicely position the force directly down on the point of the pick and reduce swinging movements. It's easiest to go into a figure four with both tools on the rock or in the ice. Hike both feet up, drop one leg over the opposite hand (left leg over right hand, see Photo 8-13), and then really tighten your abs and try to suck your weight over your wrist (see Photo 8-14). It's often helpful to get your toe stuck into something (not your other leg!) to stabilize. Practice doing figure fours on a bar or in the gym before heading outside. To release a figure four, either lift your leg all the way back around your arm and tool or, better, just release the tool if it's reasonably stable, drop your leg, and then regrab the tool.

"Figure nines" are done the same as figure fours but use the same hand and leg. They are useful for quickly moving into another reach without resetting your body.

GETTING ON ICICLES

Often the crux of mixed climbs is moving from the rock to a dangling pillar: you're pumped silly, and the ice is just out of reach. Try to get a good cam or Steinpull so that you can really reach out to the ice without your pick skating off. Failing that, a good heel hook will often allow you to keep your body tension high enough to hold the pick on the rock while you reach out to the ice. If you're getting on the very bottom of the icicle, a figure four will often give you the vertical reach and stability for the first move. Hanging one-armed from the bottom of an icicle is very strenuous; in this situation, stack one pick on the pick of the other tool, and then go into a figure four. Sometimes it's necessary to do two or three figure fours to get high enough on the ice to use your frontpoints. If the icicle is very featured, throw a heel hook with your spur into it. This takes sharp spurs but works very well.

The bottom few feet of icicles will often break off unless treated very carefully. Climbers commonly kick too hard too early because they're pumped silly, but this breaks more ice off and just makes the situation worse for everyone else who tries the route.

Be careful to keep the rope organized as you twist around to face the icicle or you may get it wrapped around your waist or neck, which makes falls complicated or painful. It's possible to turn in either direction once you have one tool in the ice. Check out which side the rope is on, and turn so that it stays organized (also see the "Free-hanging and Freestanding Ice" section in Chapter 6, Advanced Ice Technique).

CLIPPING

Clipping is one of the more dangerous moves in mixed climbing if you are still close to the ground, where falling just as you clip will mean hitting the ground. If you are clipping well above your head, you have a lot of rope in the system. For example, if you have six extra feet of rope in hand to clip, you will fall an additional 12-plus feet (see Figure 12). You may also pull out more on your tool placement if

a) Climber pulls up lots of rope in an attempt to clip the bolt from below.

b) Should he or she slip prior to clipping, the extra slack in the system could result in a dangerous fall.

20 feet

15 feet

10 feet

oops!

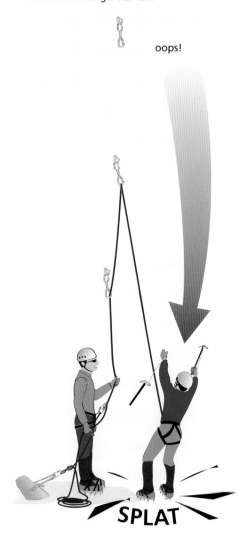

SPLAT

Figure 12. Incorrect clipping

a) Clipping when the piece is at waist level makes clipping easier and reduces the distance of any potential fall.

b) As a result, climber stops just before hitting the ground.

phew!

20 feet

15 feet

10 feet

Figure 13. Correct clipping

Photo 8-15

Photo 8-16

you are clipping too high, which can result in your tool skating off. If you have a bomber hook that will take a lot of outward pull, it makes sense to clip overhead, but if the climbing is tenuous, keep climbing until your waist is level with the bolt and clip there. If you blow the clip, you'll fall less distance (see Figure 13). This is counterintuitive but important to understand as reaching for clips is one of the more common ways to fall off a shaky edge.

Clipping with a leashed tool is often awkward: either you have to get out of the leash, which takes time, or let it dangle and risk it hitting you in the face. To clip with a leashless tool, just hook the tool across your chest and clip. (See Photo 8-15) Some climbers put Velcro on their shoulders and tools to make it less likely they'll drop their tools, but if you put the tool across your chest instead of just hanging it down from your shoulder, you'll find that it rarely or never falls off.

Alternatively, place the pick of one tool between your thumb and the grip of your other tool. (See Photo 8-16) This is surprisingly easy to do and makes clipping very fast.

Photo 8-17. Grab the rope as shown

Photo 8-19. Clip right facing carabiners with your thumb in the 'biner

Photo 8-18. Clip left facing carabiners with your middle-finger in the 'biner

Photo 8-20. Alternative "slip method"

You should be able to clip the rope in to a carabiner with a minimum of fuss and hassle. I've seen even very good climbers pump out and fall off because they can't clip quickly and efficiently. I like to hold the rope between my thumb and fingers, (Photo 8-17) pull it up, and then stick either my thumb or forefinger into the carabiner to stabilize it (Photos 8-18 and 8-19), depending on which side the gate is facing. Drop the rope into the carabiner as shown. This system removes the uncertainty of how to grab the rope, as you can clip in easily no matter which way the gate is facing. If you're wearing thick gloves, try the "slip" technique. It works well but is difficult with free-hanging carabiners (See Photo 8-20).

Because you're hanging about 18 inches below the hold your pick is on, quickdraws seem farther away at first than they normally do in rock climbing. It's especially important to climb one or two holds higher than you are used to while rock climbing to make clips efficient with ice tools. If you're reaching up extra-high to make a clip, the outward force on your tool will naturally tend to blow it off a hold.

FALLING

It's okay to take a clean fall on a good bolt, but it's much harder to take organized falls while mixed climbing than while sport climbing. Tools tend to blow unexpectedly and while loaded in odd directions, which makes it difficult to get organized in the air. Plus there are lots of sharp points whipping around. Leashless tools have the advantage that they often don't stay attached to the climber or hit him or her in the face when they blow, but on the other hand your belayer has to be awake or risk getting whacked.

Don't fall onto single ice screws or any sort of questionable gear. The whole idea behind bolted mixed climbing is to make gymnastic, wild climbing relatively safe. Falling on questionable nuts or pins is just not a good idea. If you don't feel you can climb very securely above questionable gear, retreat or get better gear. If you can't visualize yourself doing a move or falling off it safely onto good gear, retreat. Hospitals are painful and boring places to spend time. However, the old "leader must not fall" adage is definitely history on steep, well-bolted mixed climbs.

If you've got good gear close by and opt to try a low-percentage move, be ready to fall. It helps to have taken many, many falls while sport climbing. If you haven't taken a lot of falls, head to the climbing gym and do so until you're sure you can keep the rope out from behind your leg, your feet extended toward the rock or ice to absorb any impacts, and your head higher than your feet so that you don't slam in helmet first. Keeping your tools to the side, often at arm's length, is key. Most falls start when a tool or crampon blows, which usually imparts some form of sideways motion. Counter this rotation while still close to the rock or ice. This may mean pushing off with one foot or twisting in the air. If you start to contact the ice or rock before the fall is over, aggressively push away with your feet or hands rather than letting the crampons catch and spiral-fracture various bones in your lower body. Stay correctly oriented as the rope goes tight and be prepared to absorb the swing's impact. A fall doesn't end until all motion ceases.

Belaying mixed climbs requires an alert and educated belayer. For example, if you climb out onto a large icicle and fall off of it, your belayer needs to know how to catch the fall so you don't slam hard into the rock where the protection is. If there's a lot of space above the ground or any possible ledges, a relatively loose belay will kill the pendulum swing. If your belayer is an old-school climber, she will probably pull in an arm of slack, sit back on the rope, and lock the belay device.

This will accelerate your slam into the wall. Again, sport belaying teaches appropriate belaying skills.

If your belayer keeps the rope tight while you attempt to clip, the resulting rope jerk can often blow you off a delicate edge with the most rope out possible. This would be bad. On the other hand, a superloose sport-style belay is definitely not appropriate for delicate moves where a short fall will land you on an ice ledge.

TECHNIQUES FOR POPULAR MIXED ROUTES

The ice on mixed climbs is often very thin or very weak, yet it must survive multiple climbers in popular areas—treat it like fine china. If there is an existing pick hole, very delicately place your tool into the same hole and give it a gentle but firm downward pull to set it, and then treat it like a drytool edge. If you must, gently tap the head of the tool, with your other tool, into the ice for security. This tactic will set the tip of your tool and preserve the ice much better than swinging at it. I often see climbers repeatedly swinging at thin ice on a mixed route where there is already a perfectly acceptable ice hook in place. This thoughtlessness destroys the ice.

Very thin or technical ice climbing is often more akin to drytooling than ice climbing: small divots, edges, and other features become hooking holds. I've found that my confidence on thin and technical ice has increased after several years of drytooling.

CHAPTER 9

Climbers approaching the Bow Lake Headwall ice climbs, Banff National Park, Canada

Moving in the Mountains in Winter

Most ice climbs require anywhere from an hour to a day of travel time, often through hazardous terrain. Before leaving the house, check the approximate conditions of the climb you plan to attempt, the weather, and the avalanche forecast. Most of this information is available on the Web or as a recorded message on a phone.

The weather forecast is broadly useful, but I try to go climbing no matter what it says—most of the time it's at least partially wrong, and I've had a lot of great days out in the mountains when the weather was supposed to be miserable. Do change your objectives based on the forecast. For example, if the forecast is for warm temperatures and sun, consider climbing someplace shaded and higher; sun and warm temperatures aren't that great for ice climbs. On the other hand, if the forecast is for bitter cold, wind, and sunshine, head for a climb that's protected from the weather and faces south. I don't enjoy ice climbing in the shade when the temperature is below about –15°C (5°F), but this can be a very pleasant temperature in the sun. I've found that even if it's too cold to climb, the walk in can still be enjoyable, and I'm always happier with going and trying to climb than failing before I even leave the house.

Most ice climbs are in avalanche terrain to some extent, and since avalanches kill a lot of ice climbers, the avalanche forecast is a critical piece of information. Remember that the general danger level is just that; even on a day with low avalanche risk it's always possible to find the one slope that will slide. I don't venture into any sort of avalanche terrain if the danger level is above the midpoint on the scale. See Chapter 10 for more information on avalanches. If the danger is high, stick to climbs in mature trees with no hazards on the approach.

Okay, the forecast is reasonable, you've got a good climb, now the trick is getting there.

VEHICLES

This might seem like an odd section in an ice climbing book, but your vehicle is important. Be sure that the antifreeze is good to at least –30°C (–22°F); I've seen a few engines damaged from freezing fluid. A good battery is important so the rig will start on your return. After this basic maintenance, tires are the first really important consideration—studded snow tires rule. Chains are also critical if you plan to do any deep snow or off-road driving. Chains are a pain to put on and take off, but when the going gets hectic they are serious weaponry.

Most four-wheel-drive trucks are good off road. Most urban sport utility vehicles aren't

that great off road. If you're doing any serious off-road driving, respect the environment. Sometimes walking is faster and won't leave deep ruts or other evidence of your passage. If you're going for it, a winch is useful to get unstuck, but you can do a fair amount with a shovel, a pulley system, and a couple of motivated climbing friends. If you're traveling in a remote area, be sure to go in with at least one other vehicle. I've done some long walks out after ignoring this rule.

SNOWSHOES AND SKIS

If there is more than about a foot of snow on the ground and the approach is longer than about 20 minutes, snowshoes or skis are worthwhile. If the snow is really deep, the approach may be impossible without some sort of flotation assist. Snowshoes are better for desperate bushwhacking in moderate amounts of snow; skis are better for traveling long distances in more open terrain with a softer snowpack.

Any of the racy models of snowshoes are pretty much worthless for real winter travel; buy something with at least 10 inches by 30 inches of surface area or they won't support your weight on anything but hard snow—in which case you won't need them anyhow. Get a big pair of modern snowshoes and check to make sure the bindings will work with your boots—some systems seem to work only with running shoes. I like to use poles with snowshoes; they help with balance and ease suffering on steep slopes. Snowshoes with aggressive crampon-style teeth on the binding work well for windslab and brief sections of hard snow, but be careful about moving up steep snow and relying on your snowshoe crampons to hold.

Skis are a lot more fun and generally faster than snowshoes, but they do require some degree of skill to pilot. Most climbers use a short pair of skis (160cm or so) with touring or Randonee bindings. Touring bindings allow the heels to lift while skiing on the flat or up to the climb, and to lock down for descending. Before arriving in the parking lot, be sure to check that your touring binding will work on your boots. Skins work better than wax for the normally steep ascents to ice climbs, and most climbers just leave them on for the descents too. Telemark boots will work in a pinch, but they climb ice poorly, so most people change boots at the base of the climb. Look for used gear at ski swaps and consignment stores; you can usually find a decent pair of skis with bindings for about $250.

I rarely bring a map and compass with me on ice climbing trips. If I can't find the climb, the weather is probably too poor to be climbing anyhow. For obscure climbs, I'll ask a friend who has been there to show me where it is on a map, and then I'll bring the map and a GPS with the coordinates programmed into it. Since most ice climbs are by default in drainages, getting lost is seldom a real issue for ice climbers.

Whenever possible, follow the old tracks into an ice climb. This will make the going a lot easier, even if the first people wandered around erratically in the dark when they went in. Snow is hard to walk through.

OTHER SKILLS

If you are going to be traveling across glaciers and up and down mountain terrain, you need the skills to move there. These skills are broadly outside the scope of this book, but a complete winter climber should know how to self-arrest, how to travel on glaciers, and so on.

MULTIDAY CLIMBS

Spending several days on a big alpine wall is truly an unforgettable and powerful experience. Waking up high above the valley floor at first light with one full climb under your feet and another one above your head is a great feeling! There are very few pure ice climbs that take more than a day, but there are many multiday mixed or alpine climbs. A complete treatment of tactics and systems for multiday climbs is better found in books such as *Extreme Alpinism: Climbing Light, Fast, & High* by Mark Twight or the ever-popular *Mountaineering: The Freedom of the Hills*, both published by The Mountaineers Books. The following comments supplement these books.

- There is "going light" and then there is really going light. Really light means a cut-off Platypus™ for a bowl/cup, a pack that weighs under 2 pounds empty, and every other trick you can come up with to save weight. If you can halve the weight of your gear, in general you can halve the time on the route.
- In cold climates white-gas fuel is the only thing worth bringing. Pressurized gas and other fuels generally don't work when it gets cold.
- Plan and pack all the gear in a warm place the night before and leave behind anything that doesn't look essential.
- If the terrain allows it, a snow cave is a bomber, warm place to sleep. Long and skinny is better than fat and wide; make the entrance to the cave in the middle of the tube so you can shovel snow out of it faster from either end.
- Bring one big pot with a lid and something to put the stove on while it cooks so it doesn't melt down into the snow. A shovel blade works well.
- Fuel is heavy but bring enough—nothing ends a trip faster than no fuel.
- Don't bring anything extra—any "just in case" bits—except a stripped first-aid kit with pain pills.
- A good shovel is key. Black Diamond makes one that clips on to an ice tool; it's functional.
- A good sleeping bag is essential, either synthetic or down covered with waterproof breathable material; the debate rages but make sure it's warm enough so you can sleep. Not sleeping costs time.

Multiday routes are some of the most rewarding climbing I've ever done. Pick an objective, go until something stops you, retreat, learn, and try again. That's the formula for success.

CHAPTER 10

Chris Roberton on Ice Nine, Banff National Park, Alberta, Canada

Systems for Survival

The more I climb the more conservative I become. I still push hard and give a route everything I have, but to me 'winning' in the mountains means a long and safe climbing career. No one route or day out is worth my life, but the mountains are essential to my life— coming back to them again and again is the primary goal for me. It's easy to get caught up in the idea of succeeding on a route you've coveted for a long time or perhaps tried often, but each retreat means a greater knowledge base—and when success eventually comes it will be all the sweeter for past retreats! I can't tell anyone what appropriate risk is, but I do feel strongly that a successful climb means one on which nobody got hurt or rescued; summits matter little to me for this reason. My father has been a climber for 40 years; while he has never been the 'best climber,' he has survived and experienced a lifetime in the mountains.

AVALANCHES

More climbers died in avalanches from 1950 to the present than backcountry skiers; that's frightening considering how many more backcountry skiers are out there! It says a lot about the terrain we move in and perhaps our level of snow safety knowledge compared to that of backcountry skiers. An in-depth avalanche course, along with extensive reading, is absolutely essential for any serious ice climber or winter mountaineer. It's beyond the scope of this book to cover snow science in depth, but I can offer a few suggestions that I've found helpful for moving safely in avalanche terrain.

While avalanches have killed a lot of ice climbers, they have also killed a lot of professional ski guides and avalanche forecasters. These men and women are the professionals, more in touch with what causes avalanches and where not to be when they happen than anybody else. To me, this shows that making risk judgments based on even very careful snow analysis isn't all that reliable a science. I approach avalanche terrain with extreme caution and respect, and if I'm at all in doubt I run away. I've found that the more time I spend trying to understand whether a slope is safe or not, the more likely I am to ignore that first basic "Nope!" reaction and try to justify continuing. If you're not absolutely sure about a slope, then retreat unless you're very competent in assessing snow. Moving

in risky terrain for even a fantastic climb just isn't worth it for me. The following tips may help you stay alive, but they are only a small step toward safely moving in avalanche terrain.

1. Recognize what potential avalanche terrain looks like. In 1983 a lone skier died when a small (less than 30-foot) bank slid down onto him as he was skiing up a creek—he didn't recognize the danger. If you don't know you're in avalanche terrain, you can't make any sort of judgment about the situation. Any slope that's between 30 and 50 degrees with more than a few inches of snow on it can avalanche. (Slopes below 30 and above 50 degrees can also avalanche, but this is less typical.) Avalanches tend to start in wide-open areas between 30 and 50 degrees, and they can travel for long distances down gullies or

even through the woods if they are big enough.

Many ice climbs are found where water drains out from large bowls and falls over a cliff band; these bowls are the perfect place for avalanches to start. Cascade Falls in Canada is a classic example of a climb threatened by avalanche danger, as is Stairway to Heaven in Utah. Often there is no snow at the parking lot or on the sunny cliffs of Cascade, but every couple of years a party or two gets avalanched down the route. "But there was no snow on the route!" has been quoted in the newspaper more than once—the climbers couldn't recognize they were moving into danger. It can be difficult to see the terrain above your climb as you approach it in the predawn darkness, but knowing the terrain around your climb is just as important as knowing where the climb is.

As you approach an ice climb, you need to make sure that the route you're traveling is safe from ava- lanches. If you're in the bottom of a steep valley with large avalanche paths every few hundred meters, you're exposed to danger despite standing on flat ground. If the trail crosses these paths, you're exposed; if your planned climb is in the actual avalanche path, you're in danger.

2. Always get a general feel for what the snowpack is doing by checking the avalanche forecast on the phone or Web. If the climb you want to do is in the middle of an avalanche path and the risk is above low to midpoint on the danger scale, go climb something safely off in the trees with no danger on the approach. I just don't go climbing anymore when the risk is above this point; I don't think it's worth it. If the risk level is high or extreme, consider climbing only in very safe locations with absolutely no risk on the approach or at the climb— or go to the climbing gym instead.

3. Pay close attention to what's going on as you drive to your climb. With a little bit of conditioning your eyes will start to see the avalanche debris, the new fracture lines, and the texture the wind imparted to the snow as it blew in. This is all essential information. If you see a lot of new activity on south-facing slopes and you're planning a south-facing climb below a small avalanche slope, you might want to reconsider the day's plans. By constantly looking at the terrain day after day, you'll start to understand what happens during storm cycles and what that might mean to you. Observation combined with your avalanche course and reading will make you a safer climber.

4. Read or listen to the avalanche forecast every day from the start of the season, preferably for both your local area and any place you might plan on climbing that season. It's a good way to start the day. I enjoy

reading the Canadian Rockies avalanche sites, the U.S. Rockies avalanche sites, and the Utah avalanche sites over morning coffee. After reading the report, correlate what you read with what you see and experience that day. After a few seasons of doing this, you'll have a much clearer understanding of snow conditions both in your area and others you may plan to visit.

5. Ask local climbers what they think of current and past avalanche conditions on your route. The locals often have a long history with conditions on each route; if they aren't going to climb there that day, you probably shouldn't either. I often see cars with foreign license plates parked at the approach to climbs no local would dare attempt in the current snow conditions.

6. Don't be afraid to run away. If you're walking through the woods and the snow makes that unsettling whoomph noise, run away—even if the avalanche forecast says the danger is low. You're the one who has to make the call on the spot; better to be wrong and safe in the bar than wrong and dead. I've never regretted retreating off a route, even if the conditions later proved to be okay. I have really regretted being halfway up a route and hearing the big boom of a slab breaking loose somewhere in the mist overhead.

7. Watch out for small "pocket avalanches" often found in gullies and on ledges on climbs. A foot and a half of snow sliding off a 10-foot ledge may easily take you with it. I almost fell off the Weeping Wall one day when I pulled onto a snow ledge and had the whole thing rip under my feet. I ran in place and somehow managed to get a tool into the ice in time.

8. Don't assume that just because tracks lead up a slope it is safe. Those tracks may have been put in hours earlier in the day or days before when conditions were totally different. The same goes for seeing other people in the area. I once watched two large classes run for their lives at the base of a popular ice route near Chamonix. Nobody had noticed that the small slope at the top of the climb was a massive accumulation zone for blowing snow. The slope overloaded, ripped, and came down on at least 20 people—fortunately no one died, guides or clients.

Some climbers feel they will be safe once they are tied in to the rope and on the climb; the reality is that climbers have often died while tied in. Avalanches will rip screws, break ropes, or destroy the human body even if the gear holds the forces. I once had a powder avalanche go completely over a cave where I was working a mixed route; we couldn't breathe, were buffeted violently by the wind, and in general were terrified even though the actual mass of the avalanche was roaring away

Hmmm . . . Maybe time to climb something else.

from us 10 or 15 feet out in space. This encounter taught me I really don't want to get caught in a big slide—the power was just amazing. However, if it's a small slope or short gully crossing then a bomber belay may hold; I'll occasionally belay very suspect small patches of snow where the rope will swing me out to the side of a small slide.

AVALANCHE RESCUE TOOLS: BEACONS, SHOVELS, PROBES, AND AVALUNGS™

Avalanche rescue tools, such as radio beacons that are used to find a buried person, can save lives, but they do not guarantee the user will survive even a small avalanche. If you get caught in a slide large enough to bury you, the odds are immediately poor. After 15 minutes you have only a 50 percent chance of being found alive. In a larger slide, at least 30 percent of the deaths come from physical trauma. In short, by the time you're caught in a slide, the situation is grim. I've heard avalanche transceivers compared to safety belts in a car; this is a bad analogy because safety belts don't require expertise to operate and offer a lot more security than avalanche gear. Do everything you can to avoid getting caught in a slide, but if you do, having the right gear and knowing how to use it may help save your life or your partner's.

Avalanche gear works as a system: the beacon, the probe, the shovel, and someone to operate the gear. If you're buried and your partner is too, you're both in a bad position—you both may be dead by the time any rescue shows up. This is why it makes sense to cross risky slopes one at a time. A beacon without a shovel is nearly worthless; you've got to be able to dig effectively in the hard post-avalanche snow that sets up to do any good at all. A lot of ice climbers will wear a beacon but blow off taking a shovel. The beacon will help with body recovery at least, but next time you're crossing a debris pile try digging into it with an ice ax and your helmet—it just isn't effective. A probe greatly speeds up the end of the search; several manufacturers produce high-quality shovels with a probe in the handle. This is a good combination.

I prefer digital beacons, but if you practice religiously as everyone should, you can make about any beacon, including older analog models, work. However, if you practice only a couple of times a season then get a Tracker™ or Barryvox™. No matter which type of beacon you buy, check each other's signals at the trailhead, practice with them, and know that this is a last-ditch effort when your judgment fails.

The Avalung™ is a small tubelike appara-tus that allows a person to extract enough oxygen to survive for up to several hours while buried. This might be helpful in the 70 percent of avalanche accidents in which lack of oxygen is the primary cause of death. The weight and bulk of the Avalung have come down a lot in the last year or two, so it may be a valid tool for traveling in very high-risk areas, but it's still bulky for climbing. Many slides on climbs tend to bounce the climber over ice ledges and other features, making it difficult to keep the end of the tube in your mouth. I expect this technology will continue to improve radically.

Of course it is possible to travel in the backcountry without being swept away by an avalanche. This is the norm for most climbers, whether by planning or good luck. I strongly believe good luck is a product of rational judgment and knowledge; you can never have too much of either one.

BIVYING

If I have one motto that I've lived up to reasonably well in my climbing career it is this: "Back in the bar by six." Interpreted broadly, this means getting up a climb and back in 24 hours, eliminating the need to carry a sleeping bag, stove, or other piles of gear. By going light, and I mean really light, you can go faster. I have never had a forced bivy; maybe I'm not trying hard enough, but I go without bivy gear in the mountains precisely so I won't bivy. This might seem like not wearing a seat belt so you won't crash, but seat belts don't slow you down when you are moving fast. Bivy gear does. If you carry enough gear to bivy comfort-ably, you will. Instead of being hyperefficient all the time you might dawdle a bit at lunch, start an hour later, or make decisions based on the idea that a night out is okay (it is if you bring the gear). But get rid of the option of a semicomfort-able night out, and the summit is closer in terms of real physical effort required to get there and closer because a cold night out is serious motivation to keep you moving efficiently all day—or convince you to turn around early enough to prevent a miserable night. Carrying bivy gear is not safer if it means spending a very uncomfortable night out or more time exposed to risk. I plan on either going camping or going climbing for the day—however long a day is.

This doesn't mean climbing with no option of surviving a night out; sooner or later I will get caught out overnight, and I will live through the experience, but there's a big difference between spending a night out with all your toes intact and actually sleeping. I would regard a "forced" bivy as a serious error in judgment, not a glorious opportunity to suffer.

This is what I always carry in my ice pack to survive.

- A first-aid kit consisting of a roll of athletic tape, ibuprofen or stronger meds if I know how to use them, and two packs of Steri-Strips™. The Steri-Strips™ will patch up even pretty nasty cuts, the athletic tape will help make splints, and anything more serious than this means a rescue—the painkillers may help with the wait. Don't use aspirin; it's an anticoagulant. Ibuprofen is the safest according to the experts.
- A good headlamp that will last for at least 12 hours (see Chapter 1, Gear).
- A lighter. Most ice climbs are somewhere near tree line, and if I'm caught out and can at least get down to tree line, I'm going to burn something rather than freeze my feet.
- A down jacket. Not synthetic, but a good, high-quality light down jacket. The whole "warm when wet" idea is marketing hooey when it comes to insulation. You're either dry and warm or wet and not. High-quality down gives more insulation per pound than anything else.
- Food. Calories allow you to keep moving, which generates heat even if you walk in circles all night.
- A cell phone if there's any hope of cell service, and a radio if you know the frequencies and can trip the repeaters in your area. If you spend a lot of time out in the mountains, this is a very good investment.

UNINTENTIONAL BIVIES

The keys to making it through a freezing night are to reduce heat loss as much as possible by keeping insulation between you and the cold and to maximize the insulation you have or can create. I've slept in enough snow caves to know that even a shallow cave can be above freezing during a cold night, and it doesn't take much snow or effort to dig a shallow cave or pit. Sit on ropes or branches—the latter only if it's cold enough and you're willing to live with some bad karma from destroying tree limbs. Get out of the wind, either by digging a shallow snow cave/hole or hunkering down behind a rock. After you're sheltered, loosen your boots. A search-and-rescue friend of mine says he's seen many cases of bad frostbite that wouldn't have happened if the climber had simply loosened his boots fully. Take the pad out of your pack to sit on and stuff your feet into the pack. Get real close with your partner; reportedly, nothing reduces mild homophobia quicker than a cold bivy. Of course, if you can get down below tree line, then a fire is a beautiful thing. (In general I'm against fires near tree line, but if you're about to risk freezing to death, a fire is acceptable. It's not for mere comfort.)

ACCIDENTS AND RESCUES

Unfortunately, accidents are part of climbing. Some are serious enough to require a rescue, but most require just some quick first aid and an efficient retreat to civilization. Every older but active climber I know has either had a bad accident or had someone in his party seriously injured at one time or another. Are you prepared to deal with this? If not, then you have no business being in the mountains.

Most accidents don't happen cataclysmically but build slowly through a string of small errors. Perhaps your party got a late start, found the climbing a bit harder than expected, and pulled over the lip of the climb at two o'clock in the afternoon instead of ten o'clock in the morning. A few small rocks had fallen along the way, but "nothing too serious." However, just as you confidently pulled over the last bulge, a rock loosened by the warming sun fell off and found your partner's face at the wrong moment in time and space. Now what are you going to do?

Your answer to this question may save your partner's life, so take it seriously. I will climb only with partners I trust to do a competent job in the event that I need assistance. If they can't do this, then I'm essentially guiding and I reduce the risk level. This doesn't mean that I expect my partner to rescue me if I'm injured (I'm the one who made the error), but I feel safer with a capable partner. Fortunately, basic self-rescue and first aid is not that hard to figure out. If you don't know how to escape the belay and ascend safely to your partner or how to patch up basic puncture wounds, take a course. At the bare minimum, practice your rope systems and read a good book on first aid! Not having this knowledge is irresponsible at best and may be lethal to your partner at worst.

In general a self-rescue is the fastest system if the victim can function reasonably well. Unless you have the good luck to be climbing in the Alps or a few national parks in North America, mountain rescue is usually done by unpaid volunteers. Some of these groups are excellent, but most simply don't have the training or funds to pull off a high-speed, high-angle rescue. In winter the victim may well die from hypothermia waiting for the rescue. If possible, take a "Wilderness First Responder" course. This type of course will help you make a sound judgment about when to self-rescue and when to call in the cavalry. Always tell someone reliable where you are going and when you expect to return. If you don't return on time, he can launch a rescue, but only if he knows where you are. Be sure to let your reliable friend know that you are back; there's nothing worse than launching a rescue for someone who is three beers deep in the bar.

In general, if your partner can move without making his injuries considerably worse, it's good to at least get down to a sheltered spot before heading out for help, especially if the accident scene may become dangerous again (a slide gully with new slides about to come down). There are thousands of scenarios about when to leave the victim and get help or when to self-rescue and not. Only solid first-aid knowledge will enable you to make these decisions and feel good about them after the event.

I take my cell phone with me on any climb where there is cell service because I'd feel like a real idiot looking at my mangled partner and wishing I'd brought the phone. Some people feel like cell phones destroy the "wilderness experience." All I can say is that I will want the wilderness experience over with as fast as possible if I'm seriously injured—highfalutin' ethics will be secondary at that point. Know the number for the local rescue service if it's not a matter of dialing 911. Many countries in the European Alps have excellent rescue service; the cost is covered if you bought insurance, but rescue will be expensive if you didn't. Spend the $25 to $50 for insurance—it's worth it. I have a European cell phone for climbing in the Alps and other areas; North American cell phones often don't work in Europe and vice versa. In Colorado and several other states, climbers can buy "hikers and hunters" rescue insurance very cheaply (in Colorado it costs about $3 per year in 2003). This is worth having.

FIRST AID FOR CUTS AND BRUISES

Ice is surprisingly sharp, and flying ice will easily cut exposed skin. Most people get facial cuts from looking to the side as ice breaks off as they swing; ducking the helmet toward the ice is the preferred technique to avoid cuts. However, if you or a partner gets cut, here's what to do.

First try to get a good sense of how bad the cut really is, and make sure there's nothing else wrong with the victim even if he says it's just a cut. Sometimes your partner will take a hit and insist that he is "fine!" If the victim doesn't want to be examined or acts irrationally, this is a sign that the situation may be serious—don't take no for an answer. Facial and scalp cuts tend to bleed like mad for a minute or two, even if they are relatively shallow. Is the injury a cut or a blunt trauma injury? If it's a cut, how deep and how long is it? Often the impact zone on the climber's face will be numb; assure him that he hasn't just lost an entire cheek or body part and be positive in dealing with the patient. The victim needs your reassurance to stay motivated if it's a field-repairable cut, and he needs your reassurance to avoid freaking out if it is a more serious injury.

If the injury is a blunt trauma with little blood, there's not much you can do. Gently applying some snow will help reduce the swelling, but be sure not to make the patient hypothermic or freeze the skin by holding the snow in place for too long.

Fortunately, ice cuts tend to be free of debris (no gravel) and are relatively sterile.

Steri-Strips™ are generally best for closing sharp cuts. The skin has to be dry (not wet with blood or sweat) for them to stick. I often find it useful to press lightly on the cut and gently push the edges together for a minute or two to stop the blood flow before applying the strips to close the wound. Use at least two strips per inch of cut. Don't try to close the cut completely; just line the edges up as best as possible and gently pull the sides together (or have an assistant do that), then Steri-Strip it all together. You need to get to a hospital within about 4 to 6 hours for stitches to be effective, so make the decision early about whether or not to go for help. Stitches help to avoid scarring, so if your partner needs a scar-free face, getting to the hospital quickly is a good idea. If you are out for more than one day, don't completely close up the cut; often it will turn into an abscess.

When icicles break off and hit a climber on the mouth, they often punch the climber's teeth through his lip. When this happens, Steri-Strip the outside of the wounds and head for the hospital; stitches are usually required to close everything up cleanly.

More serious trauma is way outside the scope of this book. Check out *Medicine for Mountaineering* (The Mountaineers Books, 2001) for more information and take that course you've always meant to!

FROSTBITE AND HYPOTHERMIA

Severe frostbite is seldom a problem for the technical ice or mixed climber. If it's really cold, we simply retreat and come back on a warmer day. However, mild frostbite, or "frostnip," does happen, most commonly on the face and ears or hands and feet. On windy, cold days, watch your partner's face for white spots; often the victim will not feel his or her skin freezing. If you find a small patch of frostbite either on your face or your partner's, cover it up; it will hurt and feel "burned" as the blood comes back but probably be okay in the long run if you catch it early. If it doesn't look like normal flesh after it rewarms, head for the hospital. Don't rub it to bring the circulation back because this causes more damage to frozen skin.

Frostbitten feet and hands can be more serious. The first solution for cold hands or feet is to attack the root cause: the victim's core temperature has dropped, so his hands and feet are cold. Often the best solution is simply to move around, preferably toward someplace warm like the car. Movement warms up the core, pumps blood through the hands and feet, and solves the problem. Replace wet gloves with dry mitts if possible. Rewarming the cold tissue by placing the victim's hands or feet on a friendly stomach will help for the short term, but the real solution is to get the victim's whole body warm through movement.

Once an ear or other appendage is frostbitten it will tend to be susceptible to frostbite again. Frostbite forms scar tissue, which inhibits circulation. Those who have had their ears or nose badly nipped should exercise caution.

Hypothermia is potentially serious. Most ice climbers have been mildly hypothermic at a long belay on a cold day or after a dunking in an icy shower; the real problem occurs when they can't warm back up after this sort of unpleasant experience. Mild hypothermia symptoms include violent shivering, poor coordination (staggering or dropping things), slurred speech, lack of motivation, and irrationality. Again, the best solution for the early stages of hypothermia is to get moving toward a warm car. As long as the climber can still walk, he will warm up relatively quickly. Not eating sufficient calories makes one more susceptible to hypothermia, so staying well fed and hydrated is critical to preventing the experience.

If your partner becomes more severely hypothermic (stops shivering or is nonresponsive), you must get help as soon as possible. Insulate the victim as well as you can to avoid further heat loss and get help. Rewarming a seriously hypothermic patient takes skill and good facilities. Other solutions are desperate.

A LESSON

Nonclimbing magazines and media often ask me, "What's the most dangerous thing that's ever happened to you?" My usual response is, "Being born," or some other flip reply. Although climbing is dangerous, I haven't had that many superclose calls—a streak I'd like to keep going. The closest I've come to dying in an avoidable way occurred many years ago while climbing a new route with Jeff Lowe. It was the height of the ice farming era in Boulder Canyon, and there were new lines to be done everywhere. Jeff, definitely a master line spotter, saw a tenuous, beautiful two-pitch line and off we went.

The day was quite cold, maybe –20°C, and we were climbing on a single 300-foot piece of 9mm rope, used as a 150-foot double rope. This meant that I tied in to the middle with a standard bowline on a bight through my harness, but because we might need to switch ends I just backed up the "loop" with a carabiner. I led the first pitch, put on a big down jacket, and brought Jeff up. Jeff and I climbed together a fair amount back then, and at the belay he remarked that he enjoyed climbing with me because he didn't feel like I was out to kill myself—a feeling I shared about Jeff. We both had similar attitudes about gear and risk, exploration and climbing, and it was an easy partnership.

Jeff took off up the second pitch of the route, which was very thin and quite delicate, finishing in a delicate freestanding pillar, which he finessed with his usual lightness-of-being approach. The lead took a long time out of necessity, and by the time he had a solid belay I was well frozen. Rather than take my down jacket off, I kept it on and raced up to Jeff; just as I swung carefully onto the freestanding pillar the rope snaked out of my harness and up away from me. Time stopped.

Jeff yelled, "Hey!" Everything went very calm. I had been climbing fast, in second mode, so I re-placed my picks carefully. I felt the situation was tenuous enough that I didn't want to risk retying in to the rope, so I gently free-soloed the remaining few feet of the pillar with a very focused mind. So much for not trying to kill myself.

I think that when Jeff and I switched over the belay I somehow took the backup 'biner out of the loop, and the down jacket prevented me from seeing my error as the knot loosened off. I should have checked my knots and system before starting out, like I normally do, but hey, I was cold and just wanted to get moving. I now check my knots and harness on every lead—it only takes a second. I also like to look at my partner's knots and harness regularly—a quick check takes no time and is part of a good partnership. I never find it condescending when someone takes a look at my harness or knot. It shows they would like to keep climbing with me.

— *Will Gadd*

CHAPTER 11

Will Gadd on Animal Farm, the Gulag, Canadian Rockies (Photo © Andrew Querner)

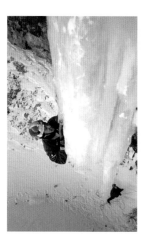

Training for Winter Climbing

Why train? Well, a fit climber will have a larger physical safety margin, climb faster, and generally have more fun than an unfit climber—reasons enough! Training, if done intelligently, also helps prevent injuries. I think the massive increase in shoulder injuries among mixed climbers is primarily due to undertraining. In theory, the best training for any sort of climbing is climbing, but ice can be hard to find on a lunch hour! The following ice-specific exercises and programs can be done at most weight rooms or climbing gyms and will make a positive difference for the performance winter climber. Remember, almost any training is better than none (as long as it doesn't cause injury), and even short sessions are better than none.

A large part of training is mental; you have to find reasons to do the workouts and satisfaction within working out or you're likely to quit before the benefits are

realized. Specific goals ("I want to climb grade six ice this winter") help, but the key ingredient to successful training is to enjoy the experience—to look forward to the workout, to be fully present during it, and to leave with the satisfaction that you worked out effectively and are making progress.

I train based on three broad principles: periodization, Specific Adaptation to Imposed Demand (SAID), and the idea that if I don't have fun then I won't train.

PERIODIZATION

I like to do a lot of different sports, so I'm usually working out in some way, but the workouts change radically based on the time of year. I keep a base fitness level through kayaking, mountain biking, running my dog, or whatever, then fine-tune my workout for specific goals or seasons. Ice/mixed climbing, unless you go to South America, is automatically a seasonal pursuit and falls naturally into a periodized program. There are many books devoted to periodized training so here's a simple but effective three-part periodization model: rest/off-season, preseason (fall), and in-season (winter). My rest/off-season is spring; I usually do some running and kayaking, but this is the time when I let all my injuries heal and rejuvenate my psyche for the coming season. In the summer I start rock climbing again, which gives a good base for ice climbing. In the fall (preseason) I start tailoring my training more specifically for performance winter climbing, and then I climb all winter with very little training. If, however, I'm stuck in Los Angeles at the Hyatt, I'll head back into the weight room and do a very ice-specific workout just to keep my fitness from degenerating; the same thing goes for periods of heavy desk work. I have climbed my best while working at least 40 hours a week on writing or other projects; a desk is only as much of an impediment to fitness as you let it be. A lot of people worry that a month off will hurt their climbing, but I always come back and climb better within a few weeks than I did before the layoff. Continuous, hard training is a sure recipe for injury and mental burnout. Periodized training gives specific fitness at specific times while allowing adequate physical and mental recovery.

SPECIFIC ADAPTATION TO IMPOSED DEMAND

Your body adapts when muscles are overloaded: gains will be made by asking more from your body than it is used to producing, then resting to let the muscle rebuild, then overloading it again. Strength is good, but it is only beneficial when it can be applied to a useful movement. For example, the ability to bench-press 300 pounds is not very relative at the top of a long ice pitch. The ability to keep swinging accurately is. Strength training for the purposes of developing non-sport-specific muscle is called body building, but many climbers seem to get stuck on the idea that strength equals performance. Rock and ice climbing demand strength that translates into upward motion.

Some sport scientists call known movements "engrams," which means a pattern that your body/mind remembers and can execute relatively efficiently. Most of the rapid initial gains from training come not from the muscles developing (they develop relatively slowly, unfortunately) but from learning the movement's engram. Today's best climbers are often not the strongest climbers but those who know how to use their strength efficiently; in other words, they are strong but that strength is transferred well through good engrams. All of the training below, with some exceptions for injury prevention, is designed to improve your body's strength in useful movements and adapt it specifically to the demands of winter climbing.

Learn to listen to your body. If you feel strong on a workout day, push hard. If you feel slow and lackadaisical in the gym (and you never know until you get there, so go when you schedule a workout), either skip the workout and just stretch or go through it at a reduced level. You're not weak mentally or a failure at working out if you feel bad in the gym; on the contrary, you're there. A slow workout is often followed in a day or two by a great one, and a large period of gains is usually followed by a slower period. This is normal; just go with it, but get into the weight room or climbing gym regardless.

EFFECTIVE TRAINING

I try to keep my workouts enjoyable by entering the gym well fueled, well hydrated, and ready to train. The pressures of office work, family, housework, or whatever can lead to missed workouts, which will make you grumpier and generally less fun to be around. You can train the people around you to encourage your workouts rather than hinder them. If you work in an office, make sure to eat something at 5:00 P.M. so you're fueled for the evening workout. In many countries where it's typical to eat late in the evening, it's common to have a tea in the late afternoon. This works well for athletes who train in the evening also.

I like to train with other motivated people, and it's a lot harder to blow off a workout when you know your partner will be there. More regular workouts give better results, which motivates me and my partners in a positive cycle. There's also a positive feeling in busting out one more lap as your partner gives you encouragement. A good partner can also critique your performance in training and offer suggestions.

Remember, if you don't have time to do all the training, do your best. Even half a workout is better than none.

FITNESS/GOAL DEFINITIONS

The following fitness levels may help define what your training requirements are or what's required to climb at a given level. These are rough levels of fitness to strive for, not absolutes.

Competent Ice: Multipitch routes up to WI 5. Aerobically fit for approaches and climbing, strong enough to do 20 one-arm pull-downs with one-quarter body weight.

WI 6 Ice: Long, hard multipitch routes done quickly. Aerobically fit for long days, strong enough to climb hard ice all day, able to do 20 one-arm pull-downs with half body weight and hold a one-arm lockoff briefly.

M8/Difficult Mixed: Short, difficult climbs. Can hold a half-lever for 5 seconds and do five one-arm pull-downs with three-quarters body weight.

M12/Competition: High-level mixed or competition climbing. Able to hold a front lever for 10 seconds, do 10 one-arm pull-downs with three-quarters body weight, and hold a one-arm lockoff for 10 seconds.

TRAINING SCHEDULES

The volume of training required for results depends on what the desired results are. If you want to climb a beautiful four-pitch grade four more enjoyably, a couple of workouts a week will be enough. If you want to climb 300 meters of vertical ice in a morning or M12, stock the fridge with enough calories to feed a family of four and clear your schedule. The charts below outline the realistic weekly time requirements for different levels of fitness. Workouts can definitely be combined, but most people will work out most effectively for relatively short periods. I find that after a couple of hours of hard training I'm done—make your workout time count.

Each number in the charts below represents the number of times in a week to hit a specific set of exercises. For example, if you are strength training for M12, you go twice a week.

WORKOUT THEORY

Start by taking a good hard look at what your strengths and weaknesses are: the goal is to balance these out. Most people would rather train their strengths than their weaknesses. For example, if you are very flexible and aerobically fit but lack any sort of power, it's more fun to train for flexibility than do the strength exercises, but this is less productive. It's initially more fun to train for what we are good at than what will actually improve our climbing. If you can do one-arm pull-ups but can't hang on to an ice tool, spend proportionately more time training on an ice tool. The ability to do a one-arm pull-up is useless if you can't hang on to the tool!

Strength exercises are designed to overload specific muscles. Examples are front levers, Peg-Board workouts, and all exercises done in the gym. These are done at most twice a week and in combination with applied movement workouts.

Off-Season (late summer, no ice)

Goal	Strength Hours per week	Climbing/ Gym	Aerobic Training Hours Per week	Total Time/Week
Competent Ice	1	2 (Two-hour sessions)	3+	8+ hours
WI 6 Ice	1–2	3 (Two-hour sessions)	4+	10+ hours
M8	1	3 (Three-hour sessions)	About 2	12+ hours
M12/Competition	2	3 (Three-hour sessions)	Not more than 3	14 hours

Preseason (late fall, some ice formed and accessible, 8-hour days on weekends)

Goal	Strength Hours per week	Climbing Gym	Ice/Mixed/Drytooling Day-long sessions per week	Aerobic Training Hours per week	Total Time/Week
Competent Ice	1	1	1	3+	12 hours
WI 6 Ice	1	2	2	3	20+ hours
M8	2	2	2	To Climbs, 2 if time	24+ hours
M12/Comp.	1	1	3	To Climbs, 2 if time	30+ hours

In-Season

Goal	Strength Hours per week	Climbing Gym	Ice/Mixed/Drytooling Day-long sessions per week	Aerobic Training Hours per week	Total Time/Week
Competent Ice	1	2	2	3	12 hours
WI 6 Ice	1	2	2–3	3	20 hours
M8	1	3	2–3	To Climb	24+ hours
M12/Comp.	0	1	4	To Climb	40 hours

Note that for each training category the emphasis early season is on building strength, then transitioning that strength to the outdoors, then climbing well through the season while maintaining that strength. This is basic periodization. I'm assuming that competent ice climbers will have one or two days per week to climb all day, grade six ice climbers two days a week, M8 climbers two mixed days a week, and M12/competition climbers all the time they need to train and climb.

Always warm up before training—10 easy minutes on the treadmill or rowing machine, easy traversing on the bouldering wall, or jumping up and down in place—whatever it takes to get loose. The idea is to get your muscles warmed up and ready to go. If there's no treadmill, or other options, do whatever exercise you're about to attempt, at a very reduced capacity; for example, doing lat pull-downs with less than half the amount of weight you plan to use during your workout. Break a sweat before going all-out; it will give you a better workout with less chance of injury.

WEIGHT ROOM EXERCISES

All exercises in the weight room should be done with clean form; you can use more weight or do more reps if you use lousy technique, but the idea is to train the muscles hard, not bang on tendons and ligaments. Good clean form will mean lighter weights. What counts is the amount of load you're putting on the muscles, not the size of the weight. Let the disc-heads in the gym laugh at you using light weights, but your goal is performance, not ego fulfillment.

A set is defined as doing an exercise until near failure on the last rep. If you're not increasing the weight over time, then you're staying at the same level, not gaining.

One-arm Pull-downs

Goal: Simulate the motion of pulling up and locking off on an ice tool. Doing these one-handed greatly increases the number of

One-arm pull-down A

One-arm pull-down B

One-arm pull-down C

muscles involved and very closely mimics real climbing. Low reps are for power, high reps for power endurance.

Switch the two-handed pull-down bar to a one-handed bar. Most gyms have these on the double-sided cable machine.

Start with your arm and shoulder fully extended, then smoothly pull the handle down into a full lockoff. Slowly release the weight back to maximum arm extension, then smoothly pull it down again. Jerking with your back to snap the weight down is bad form. Do one arm, then switch arms, take a 1- to 2-minute rest, repeat. For an even more specific workout, reach upward with the free hand while locked off at the bottom of the move.

Front lever (I'm sagging too much in this photo!)

Half-lever

Front Levers

Goal: Front levers were first popularized by John Gil, and they are an amazing way to gain core strength for mixed climbing. Keeping your feet on holds is much harder with crampons than rock shoes; having good core strength will really help!

Hang straight-armed from a pull-up bar with your hands slightly wider than shoulder-width apart. Slowly and without swinging, pull your body up until it is horizontal to the ground. Hold this position for a few seconds, then return to a hanging position. Kicking is not allowed, nor is swinging. The idea is to control the swing and develop your strength.

Half-levers

Goal: Same as front lever.

Hang as for a front lever and move into a front lever but with one leg pulled back to reduce the amount of weight. This is an excellent way to start front-lever training!

Curl-ups

Goal: Gain core strength.

If you're just starting out to gain core strength, front levers and half-levers will be impossible. Curl-ups start the process. Hang as for a front lever, but pull your knees up to your chest before rotating them up to the bar. Every little kid has done these; it may just take some time to get back into shape!

Hammer Swings

Goal: Develop your deltoids, triceps, and forearms for swinging a tool. Also strengthen your shoulder to avoid injury.

Tool version: Tape a couple of half-pound weights (rocks, cans of beer) to each

Curl-up

tool, raise your elbow to near your ear with the tool hanging down your back, then slowly swing it up over your head as though climbing. Be as precise and smooth as possible. The goal here is to develop the strength and coordination for swinging a tool; letting it flop around does not help. This exercise is incredibly, violently pumping but will help maintain your swing's efficiency on long pitches!

Dumbbell version: Take a light dumbbell in each hand, but grab the bar

Hammer swing A

Hammer swing B

near one disc. Bring it up over your head as though swinging, and flick it at the top of the arc.

Shoulder Training

Goal: Goal: Develop the shoulder muscles for hanging straight-armed (one-arm pull-downs, staggered pull-ups), swinging (see

Internal rotation

External rotation

Dips A

Dips B

Hammer Swings above), and to prevent injury (Internal and External Rotation). Do three sets of 15–30 for each exercise.

Shoulder injuries are increasingly common among mixed and ice climbers. The main mechanisms of injury are landing on the shoulder violently at full arm extension and repetitive injuries from swinging a tool. The rotator cuff is a group of four muscles (subscapularis, supraspinatus, infraspinatus, and teres minor) that helps lift your arm up over your head and also rotate it toward and away from your body. If you participate in racquet sports or throwing sports, you may already have found out about your rotator cuff. These exercises are quick as they involve relatively small movements.

Dips

Goal: Develop triceps and pectoral strength, essential for pressing down on a tool as you move up. Also good to make sure the "antagonist," or opposing, muscles are well trained to prevent imbalances.

Most gyms have a dip stand. I like to be able to do the same number of dips as I can pull-ups, again with good clean form. Most climbers will be weak at this exercise to start, but strength comes quickly.

Staggered Pull-ups

Goal: Develop power for pulling up on ice tools.

Hang a piece of webbing off a pull-up bar, then hang from the bar and webbing and pull up!

Staggered pull-ups A

Staggered pull-ups B

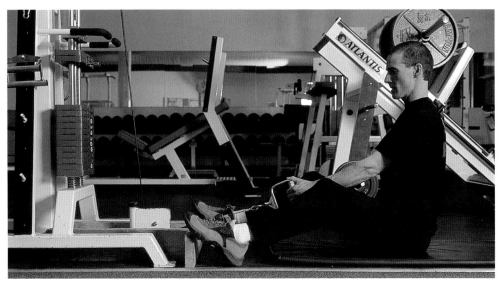

One-arm rows A

One-arm rows B

One-arm Rows

Goal: Develop the latisimus, back, long head of the triceps, and biceps in combination for climbing.

Grab one handle of the cable row machine and smoothly pull it to full lockoff. Don't "throw" the weight with your back, but keep your back straight up and down through the entire exercise. You'll feel every muscle in your upper body contract at some point during this exercise; it's excellent training for ice and rock climbing!

Calf Stands

Goal: Reduce the amount of calf pain and suffering involved on long pitches while improving balance.

Find a stair, rock, or curb and, if possible, put your boots on. Doing this exercise in any shoes works; I just like to do it in my boots. Put the tip of the boot on the edge with your heel hanging out over the dropoff, then stand one-legged on it until you either lose your balance or start to pump out. Switch feet and repeat until your calves are as big as your head. I like to slowly raise and lower my heel while staying balanced; this move closely resembles real climbing.

CLIMBING GYM/GARAGE MOVEMENT EXERCISES

The best summer preparation for ice or mixed climbing is rock climbing; anybody who can lead 5.10 can follow any pure ice pitch after only a few days out. Leading ice is a very different game, but rock fitness translates very well to basic ice fitness—plus rock climbing is a lot more fun than chucking weights!

Peg-Board

Build a simple Peg-Board for ice-tool use. These are made from a 2 by 12 board about 6 feet long with holes drilled about every foot. Train only while still strong enough to use the board smoothly. Excessive jerking and flailing is bad for your shoulders and tendons.

Goal: Build power for lockoffs and other intense moves while training your hand/eye coordination to use small placements.

Beginning version: Pull up on both

Peg-Board workout

tools, lock off, reach the next hole, repeat. Come down smoothly.

Advanced version: Start with both tools in the two bottom holes; lock off, and reach up to a hole at full lock off. Pull up on the high tool while pushing on the lower tool. Lock off, and release the lower tool; reach high and lock off again. Repeat.

For the first few weeks of a Peg-Board routine, it will be entirely sufficient to do this once a week. As you build strength, you can increase the routine to twice a week, but only as long as you can do the movements smoothly. After you are strong enough to go up and down the board once, increase the number of laps.

Jug Climbing with Lockoffs

Goal: Build full-body strength and awareness for climbing on steeper ground.

Pick a gently overhanging wall with good jugs, either bouldering or top-roped. Start one-handed on a good jug, pull up into a lockoff, reach up to another jug but hold the position for at least 5 seconds, then grab it. The 5 seconds simulates the amount of

Anti-swing training A

Anti-swing training B

Anti-swing training C

time it would take to get another placement. Repeat all the way up the wall, down-climb, and do another lap until you're flamed.

Anti-Swing Training

Goal: Develop core abdominal and back strength for keeping your feet on during steep climbs.

Find a steep bouldering cave with good holds. Start in the back on good holds, drop your feet while keeping swing to a minimum, put them back on, make a small move to another good hold, drop your feet, put them back on, grab a new hold, repeat!

Shoulder Roll and Lock

Goal: Develop your ability to shoulder-roll on steep terrain.

Start hanging by two hands with your feet about level with your shoulders and your feet supported by a chair or something solid. Pull your chest to the bar, roll one shoulder up and into a lockoff, release one hand and extend it upward, come back down to start with two hands. This can also be done using ice tools. Wicked exercise for mixed climbing!

Ice Tool Hangs

I have yet to find any exercise that builds the specific strengths of hanging off an ice tool other than hanging off an ice tool. For training I prefer an older set of ice tools with no major pinky rest or leashless grip. Take the leashes off and prepare to get pumped silly. Tape the picks up really well and most gyms will let you do this on their pull-up bar.

Single-tool hangs: Hang straight-armed off one tool for as long as possible. Gloves are critical to prevent blisters. It doesn't matter what kind you use; the goal is to work the forearms. Hang off one tool until failure, grab it with the other, and repeat until you simply can't hang on for even a few seconds. This is an absolutely brutal exercise; you may be able to hang onto the tool for only a few seconds; this is okay. The goal is to develop power.

Double-tool intervals: Hang off both tools for 20 seconds, rest for the same amount of time as you hung, repeat until satisfactorily pumped.

One-handed figure fours: Hang straight-armed off a leashless ice tool, then bust into a figure four. This is a sick exercise but very applicable to hard mixed climbing.

Drytooling Indoors—Circuits and Bouldering

Drytool training is an effective way to increase forearm strength regardless of whether you climb leashed or not. If you can drytool well, you can also dramatically increase your security and forearm resiliency on ice.

All you need for a good drytooling workout is a 4 by 8 piece of plywood in a frame with plastic, wooden, or rock holds bolted on. If you climb leashless, then train leashless; for a really good pump, train leashless on old-school tools with no grip enhancers.

I like to set a 10-move or so circuit and do it until I develop a really good pump.

Drytool training

Rest a minute, repeat. There are a hundred variations on this basic program; the goal is to specifically train forearm endurance in combination with the rest of your body. I like to circuit train because I can measure my gains by the number of moves I can do.

Drytooling Outdoors—Laps

Goal: Develop endurance and drytool-specific engrams. This exercise is also excellent for the pure ice climber.

Find a cliff that flat-out isn't good for rock climbing (road cuts, quarries, buildings, an old silo) and hang a top-rope on it. Run laps wearing crampons and using your normal tools; again, I like to train leashless on old-school tools without grip enhancers. If you are climbing leashless, make sure to also train some laps with your leashless tools; the geometry is often different and the goal here is to develop your drytooling skills.

Stretching

There are two main reasons to stretch and increase one's flexibility: increased movement range (appreciated when stemming to a far-off icicle) and less muscle resistance within a movement. There is little evidence for injury prevention or direct performance improvement, but increased and more efficient range of motion are good enough reasons. Check out *Stretching* by Bob Anderson (Shelter, 2000) for a full routine. I've found that gentle, long-duration (up to 3 minutes) stretches produce the best results for me, but keep track of your range of

Some favorite stretches

motion and do what works for you. I always work through my range of motion as part of my warm-up on the climbing wall; this also produces results and seems less tedious than lying on the floor. Yoga is also very good for results (plus you can do it with your partner/family). Most of the stretches I do come from martial-arts books; these guys have a dynamic range of flexibility and strength through that range, the same goal as climbers have. If one type of stretching doesn't work for you, try something else; stretching is a very body-specific exercise. Be sure you are actually increasing your range of motion; too many stretching programs fail to produce any results.

On-Ice Training

All of these top-rope training exercises will improve your climbing radically if practiced regularly with focus.

Hang a top-rope on about 60 feet of the steepest ice you can find, preferably something with curtains or other features to play on. Even 20 feet of near-vertical ice is enough to work with (road cuts work fine).

1. **Minimizing "sticks" or tool placements.** Climb the top-rope once as you normally would (see the "Putting It Together: Tracking" section in Chapter 3, Basic Ice Climbing) and count your total number of placements, then climb it using as few tool placements as possible. Focus on making the maximum possible distance between each placement and making each placement bomber. Falling off is bad form. The goal here is to make the climb "shorter" as defined by the total number of placements required. This is an exaggerated way of learning how to make fewer but solid placements.

2. **Minimal swinging.** Climb the route again using as few swings as possible; this means hooking as much as possible and being very careful and analytical about where each tool placement should go. This will force you to really think about how ice fractures, what kind of ice gives good placements, and how to swing at various ice consistencies. Really play with the bare minimum for a stick, or placement; falling off with a good tight top-rope is encouraged. Only by going too far will you learn how far is far enough. Count swings for your partner, and look at how she moves.

3. **Speed.** Climb the route as quickly as possible, going full-out with no regard for security. Belay with a Grigri™; the belayer may need a backup person when the times get really fast! Switch off with your partner, and critique each other's technique and speed. Break out the stopwatch: a fast time on a 60-foot vertical piece of ice is 30 seconds or less going all out. At a world-cup level, the time may be under 20 seconds. Do at least a half-dozen or more laps; you'll be amazed at much faster you start to climb and at how reasonable the ice starts to seem

compared to the first run (see "Big Routes: Modern Tactics for Speed and Warmth" in Chapter 3, Basic Ice Climbing, for different tactics). This exercise will radically speed up your time when seconding a pitch.

4. **Climbing without swinging.** Most routes can be climbed without swinging the ice tools at all. This exercise is best done on a piece of ice that has already seen a lot of traffic (do the above exercises first and then try this on the same line), but it will work on most any piece of ice.

5. **Climbing without kicking.** Good ice climbers use the natural features of the ice as a rock climber would. Place the crampons in the natural holes, stand on small edges, and look each time you place a crampon. This exercise will really help increase the solidity of your crampons by forcing you to look at them each time and choosing locations that already have a "hold" half-made.

6. **Laps with no crampons.** Climbing without crampons is a lot easier than it would seem at first. This exercise teaches you how to climb smoothly. It will also help you to be far more conscious of the ice features and understand how different body positions affect the forces underfoot.

7. **Laps with a pack.** In general the leader should have only a very light pack containing a belay jacket and spare mitts, which means that the second may have some weight.

Climbing a pitch of near-vertical ice with a 20-pound pack is a lot harder than climbing it without one! This exercise is a strength exercise to some extent, but it also teaches you how to climb with weight on your back. Try doing laps back to back with a very heavy (40-pound) pack for a real burn or with a tool with no leash on it.

8. **Laps with one tool then no tools.** Most climbers place far too much emphasis on their tools and not enough on staying balanced over their feet. Climb the pitch with one tool, then try it with no tools. You'll be surprised how much you can do, especially with a good pair of dexterous gloves to grab "ice holds."

9. **Ice-screw placement.** Climb the pitch placing a full rack of eight to 10 screws, then have your partner climb it and critique your placements while removing the screws. Switch roles. This exercise is absolutely invaluable for learning how to place solid screws efficiently. Most leaders wait until they are on lead to play with different tactics and ideas; it's far better to do this on top-rope first. A good leader puts in good screws quickly; a good second climbs fast, takes the screws out efficiently, and cleans them well. This exercise hones these skills. Also try out slinging large icicles, I-threads, and all the other tricks. One day spent doing this can be better than 10 leads. See the "Placing Ice Protection"

section in Chapter 4, Anchors, Belaying, and Leading, on how to place an ice screw.

10. **Laps with no leashes on traditional tools.** This is a great way to get pumped silly. Add a pack for bonus value.

AEROBIC TRAINING

Many climbers don't realize the importance of aerobic training for ice climbing; a fit climber may not necessarily arrive at the climb any faster (in fact, going slow is good), but she will arrive fresher and better able to succeed on the climb. Long ice routes can take up to 18 hours car to car. Even 30-minute approaches can do damage to your climbing ability if you don't have reasonable fitness. The quantity of aerobic training necessary will be in direct relation to the style of climbing you do. Long, multipitch routes almost invariably have long approaches. The ability to arrive at the climb relatively fresh is essential.

If possible, buy a heart-rate monitor. Not only will it help you train more effectively but it's fun to watch what's going on in your body. There are many books written on different aerobic training schemes; I find that just getting out the door and moving three to six times a week works well. I train at a relatively slow heart-rate, about one-half to two-thirds of my max; this means walking up any hills and often going at a pace that seems very slow. A good rule of thumb is that if you can't breathe solely through your nose, you're probably going too fast. Many people train too hard aerobically and lose motivation; this makes all your workouts less fun.

Mix up your workouts. The main thing is to get your heart beating for an hour or so. I bike, run, or hike up hills with a pack depending on the day. If I'm training for a really big climb or link-up, I increase the hours of aerobic training and decrease my strength training. A good rule is that if you plan to have 14-hour days on the weekends, you need to train aerobically at least 7 hours each week. I find that "big-day" fitness is difficult to get by anything other than going out for big days, but those big days can be made a lot more comfortable by regular, shorter workouts. If, on the other hand, you're going to hike 10 minutes to a mixed crag, all you need is general aerobic fitness; three 30- to 45-minute sessions a week will be enough.

Competent Ice—Preseason Example						
Monday	**Tuesday**	**Wednesday**	**Thursday**	**Friday**	**Saturday**	**Sunday**
Rest/Light Aerobic	Strength	Rest	Strength	Rest	Climbing	Climbing
Gym Movement	Stretch	Aerobic	Stretch	Aerobic/Stretch	Aerobic to climb	Aerobic to climb

Surprisingly, most of the benefits in aerobic training come from regular sessions of more than 15 minutes.

SAMPLE ROUTINES

Three routines are described below for different styles of climbing. The ideas for sets and combinations are only ideas; you'll have to play with what your body can handle and how much time you have. Notice that the workouts focus primarily on strength in the gym or weight room and endurance in the outdoors. I've always found climbing endurance is best developed through climbing; weight-room endurance does not broadly translate to climbing endurance. As you get stronger, you can add more sets, more exercises, and more repetitions. The main thing is to work out regularly and with focus.

COMPETENT ICE: (PRESEASON)

Strength Workout

First, warm up, then:

One-arm pull-downs: Three sets of 20 repetitions, whatever weight you can do. This may mean starting at one weight and then dropping the weight each set.

Peg-Board: If you're strong enough to do the Peg-Board workouts (assuming you have access to one), this is the preferable exercise. One to three sets of each Peg-Board exercise.

Hammer swings: Four sets of 40-plus reps on each arm. Pick a weight that allows you to do this.

Shoulders: Three sets of 20–30 of lateral raises and external rotators.

One-arm rows: Three sets of 10.

Dips: Three sets of whatever you can do per set.

Calf stands: As described in the "Weight Room Exercises" section.

Levers: Use whatever lever exercise you can do five reps of, three sets.

Jug lockoffs: This is harder, but if you can do sets with 10–15 lockoffs, the wall is about right. The idea is to primarily work your shoulders, not your hands, although they'll get a good workout too.

Ice tool hangs: Two sets of double-tool interval hangs (go until you're failing in only a couple of seconds, rest for 5 minutes, repeat). Get a really good pump on!

WI 6—Late Fall Example						
Note this workout assumes you already have a good base and have access on the weekend to enough ice to train on.						
Monday	**Tuesday**	**Wednesday**	**Thursday**	**Friday**	**Saturday**	**Sunday**
Aerobic—as needed	Strength	Aerobic—	Strength Two hours	Rest	Climbing—Long Route	Climbing—Lap Workout
Gym Movement	Gym Movement	Stretch	Stretch	Aerobic/ Stretch	Aerobic to climb	Aerobic to climb

Mixed Training—Late Fall Example						
Note the main difference between climbing at an M8 and competition level will be in volume, and this depends on how fit you are. The idea is to walk out of the gym knowing you pushed as hard as you could and need a rest day.						
Monday	**Tuesday**	**Wednesday**	**Thursday**	**Friday**	**Saturday**	**Sunday**
Aerobic— as needed	Strength	Aerobic— 30 minutes	Strength	Rest	Climbing— Drytool Training	Climbing— Lap Workout
Gym Movement	Gym Movement	Stretch	Aerobic to climb	Stretch	Aerobic to climb	Aerobic/ Stretch

Climbing Training

Drytool exercises: Do them if you have access to the terrain; otherwise, gym climbing or real climbing on steeper routes with good holds. Steep cracks are also excellent.

WI6 (LATE FALL)
Strength Workout

First, warm up, then:

One-arm pull-downs: Two sets of 10 repetitions, two sets of 20 reps.

Or:

Peg-Board: If you're strong enough to do the Peg-Board workouts (and assuming you have access to one), this is the preferable exercise. Two to five sets of each Peg-Board exercise.

Hammer swings: Four sets of 40-plus reps on each arm. Pick a weight that allows you to do this.

Shoulders: Four sets of 10 each, lateral raises and external rotators.

One-arm rows: Two sets of six, two sets of 15.

Dips: Four sets of whatever you can do per set.

Calf stands: As described in the "Weight Room Exercises" section.

Levers: Use whatever lever exercise you can do five reps of, three sets.

Jug lockoffs: Four sets of 15–20 lockoffs each side per set.

Ice tool hangs: A few sets of single-handed hangs, then at least 20 minutes of double-handed hangs.

Climbing Training

Drytool exercises: Do them if you have access to the terrain during the week.

Lap training day (Sunday in the above schedule): Do at least 500–1000 feet of climbing on top-rope, playing with the different games.

MIXED CLIMBING (LATE FALL)
Strength Workouts

I like to split my strength workouts into two workouts, one in the weight room and one in the climbing gym/garage.

Workout One

First, warm up!

Staggered pull-ups: Three sets of whatever takes you to failure.

One-arm pull-downs: Four sets of 5–10 reps, done with 2- to 3-minute rests between sets.

Hammer swings: Four sets of 40-plus reps on each arm. Pick a weight that allows you to do this.

Shoulders: Four sets of 10 each, lateral raises and external rotators.

One-arm rows: Two sets of 10, two sets of 15.

Dips: Five sets of whatever you can do.

Workout Two

Peg-Board: Two to five sets of each Peg-Board exercise.

Levers: Five sets of one to five reps, starting with front levers and moving down to curl ups as your strength fades.

Jug lockoffs: Four sets of 15–20 lockoffs each side per set, or to failure.

Shoulder rolls: Three to five sets of reps to failure.

Anti-swing training: Hard to set specific reps, but you'll figure out your own limits quite quickly.

Ice tool hangs: First try to bust into a one-handed figure four. If you can't do this one-handed, do it two-handed to learn the motion. Then do a couple sets of single-handed hangs to failure.

Climbing Training

Drytool laps: Three to five circuit sets to failure.

Drytool intervals: Do a lap, rest for a minute, repeat until desperately pumped.

Lap training day (Sunday in the above schedule): Do at least 500–1000 feet of climbing on top-rope, playing with the different games.

THE GOLDEN RULE

Snap! I just did what everyone always told me never to do: "Never fall while leading ice." I've preached these words enough myself; in a sport without rules I broke one.

When I first heard those words eight years ago it was explained to me that if you do fall, "You will likely break your ankles when your crampons hit the ice, and you will probably stab yourself with one of your tools."

Since that day a lot has changed in my life. I started climbing full time, and I especially fell in love with ice climbing. The past four winters I have climbed water ice 50 to 60 days of each year. I spent the first four years climbing occasionally, maybe 10 to 20 days a season, and I paid my dues. I advanced slowly: first doing all the grade threes, then the fours, and then the fives. When I started climbing grade six it was easy for me. I had been to "school" and the progression seemed logical. I have spent the last couple years doing a lot of mixed climbing and the ice is always fun but always the easy part. "It's only ice; how hard can it be?"

The reason we climb ice is not because it's hard. We climb ice because it is committing, visceral, and meditative. In the three weeks leading up to my fall I had done more hard, committing ice climbing than ever. I had climbed over 2000 meters of ice and mixed terrain, in an alpine setting, with the easiest pitches going at WI 5—and most quite a bit harder. Only a few days earlier I had soloed a 200-meter VI, WI 6. I had the confidence and the skills, but what I had also gained was complacency.

Complacency kills! It has no place in the mountains. If you get lazy in the mountains, you will pay dearly. Until this moment I had never fallen on ice, but I had fallen many times in the winter while leading mixed climbs. I took falls off of thin technical ice onto bolts. I had taken several falls when the pillar I was climbing snapped. As long as I was dangling in midair there was not much to worry about. I had also seen and heard of many ice climbing falls where the outcome was fine and the stories were classic. Maybe I started to doubt the validity of the "Golden Rule."

When this accident happened I was doing something no more technical or committing than my guide let me do on my first day of ice climbing. I was bouldering no more than 10 feet off the deck on grade four ice. However, there were a few things I wasn't thinking about: it was cold, the ice was brittle, I was traversing (which always sucks with ice tools), and most importantly I was bored. My tools popped, I jumped off and landed on my feet, but when you do that with crampons on your feet, it's trouble. Goodbye ankle, hello crutches. Hello eight months of physiotherapy, goodbye climbing goals.

"OK," I thought, "so I broke my ankle. I learned my lesson and will be back in six weeks." Think again! Let me tell you a little something about ankles. Ankles are very complicated joints: they are hard to stay off of, they take a lot of abuse, and they have chronically low blood flow, resulting in slow healing times. I have since heard of many climbers who have ended their careers because they broke their ankles while falling on ice. Many of the falls were while bouldering or soloing easy ground. Many of the climbers were extremely talented. All fell victim to complacency.

So in this day and age of falling on mixed climbs and thinking that "ice is the easy part," stay focused, respect your environment, show respect for your sport. Keep your picks, mind, and body sharp. Keep preaching and living by the Golden Rule. Ice climbing is the easy part only when you're not falling!

— *Rob Owens*

Index

About the Author

Will Gadd

Ice climbing has changed dramatically in the last five years, and Will Gadd has been a major part of the ice and mixed revolution. Gadd started climbing with his parents before he could walk and, thirty-some years later, continues to spend at least 100 days a years tied into a rope. He climbed his first frozen waterfall more than 20 years ago but never stopped learning and experimenting with winter climbing. In the last ten years he has opened many new ice and mixed routes all over the world, including the first M9-M12 routes. For the last five years he has taught ice climbing clinics around the world; this book shares his systems for safety, speed, training, hard routes and the joy of climbing anything frozen. He hopes it will help any novice or expert climber find new ways to look at winter climbing.

About the Photographer

Self-taught photographer Roger Chayer currently lives in Calgary, Alberta but his freelance work has taken him around the world. With the Canadian Rockies in his backyard, however, it isn't surprising that adventure sport and landscape photography dominate his portfolio. A climber and outdoor sport enthusiast, Roger has an inherent ability to capture the true essence of the action and locales depicted in his images. His photographs have been published in magazines such as *Climbing, Rock and Ice, Outside, Explore, Gripped, Alp* (Italy), and *Climber* (UK). To learn more about Roger's work, please visit his website at *www.rogerchayer.com.*

Roger Chayer

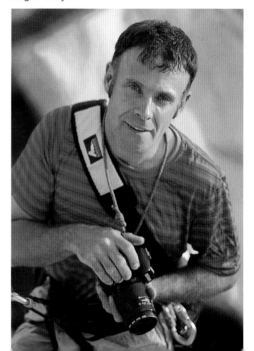

THE MOUNTAINEERS, founded in 1906, is a nonprofit outdoor activity and conservation club whose mission is "to explore, study, preserve, and enjoy the natural beauty of the outdoors. . . . " Based in Seattle, Washington, the club is now the third-largest such organization in the United States, with 15,000 members and five branches throughout Washington State.

The Mountaineers sponsors both classes and year-round outdoor activities in the Pacific Northwest, which include hiking, mountain climbing, ski-touring, snowshoeing, bicycling, camping, kayaking and canoeing, nature study, sailing, and adventure travel. The club's conservation division supports environmental causes through educational activities, sponsoring legislation, and presenting informational programs. All club activities are led by skilled, experienced volunteers who are dedicated to promoting safe and responsible enjoyment and preservation of the outdoors.

If you would like to participate in these organized outdoor activities or the club's programs, consider a membership in The Mountaineers. For information and an application, write or call The Mountaineers, Club Headquarters, 300 Third Avenue West, Seattle, WA 98119; 206-284-6310.

The Mountaineers Books, an active, nonprofit publishing program of the club, produces guidebooks, instructional texts, historical works, natural history guides, and works on environmental conservation. All books produced by The Mountaineers Books fulfill the club's mission.

Send or call for our catalog of more than 500 outdoor titles:

The Mountaineers Books
1001 SW Klickitat Way, Suite 201
Seattle, WA 98134
800-553-4453
mbooks@mountaineersbooks.org
www.mountaineersbooks.org

The Mountaineers Books is proud to be a corporate sponsor of Leave No Trace, whose mission is to promote and inspire responsible outdoor recreation through education, research, and partnerships. The Leave No Trace program is focused specifically on human-powered (nonmotorized) recreation.

Leave No Trace strives to educate visitors about the nature of their recreational impacts as well as offer techniques to prevent and minimize such impacts. Leave No Trace is best understood as an educational and ethical program, not as a set of rules and regulations.

For more information, visit *www.LNT.org* or call 800-332-4100.

ALSO IN THE MOUNTAINEERS OUTDOOR EXPERT SERIES:

Climbing: Expedition Planning, *Clyde Soles & Phil Powers*

Climbing: Training for Peak Performance, *Clyde Soles*

Climbing: From Gym to Crag, *S. Peter Lewis & Dan Cauthorn*

OTHER TITLES YOU MIGHT ENJOY FROM THE MOUNTAINEERS BOOKS:

Mountaineering: The Freedom of the Hills, *The Mountaineers*
The classic mountaineering text since 1961, *Freedom* has instructed and inspired more than half a million climbers the world over.

Medicine for Mountaineering & Other Wilderness Activities, *James Wilkerson, M.D.* A classic since 1967, this book starts where most first-aid manuals stop. Written and edited by a team of climber-physicians, this is the perfect companion to *Mountaineering: The Freedom of the Hills.*

Extreme Alpinism: Climbing Light, Fast, & High, *Mark Twight & Jim Martin*
This master class centers on climbing the hardest routes with little gear and the most speed.

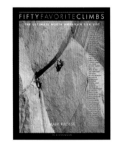

Fifty Favorite Climbs: The Ultimate North American Tick List, *Mark Kroese*
Fifty elite climbers share their favorite routes—a celebration of contemporary climbing history and the climbers who have shaped it.

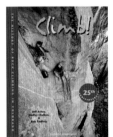

Climb! The History of Rock Climbing in Colorado,
Jeff Achey & Dudley Chelton.
25th anniversary edition of a cult classic that profoundly changed the world of rock climbing.

Available at fine bookstores and outdoor stores, by phone at 800-553-4453 or on the Web at *www.mountaineersbooks.org*